PAUL KEELS'S

Tales from the

BUCKEYES'
CHAMPIONSHIP SEASON

Director of production: Susan M. Moyer
Project manager: Tracy Gaudreau
Developmental editor: Gabe Rosen
Copy editor: Cynthia L. McNew
Dust jacket design: Christine Mohrbacher
All photos courtesy of AP/WWP

ISBN: 1-58261-539-X

Printed in the United States

Sports Publishing L.L.C.
www.sportspublishingllc.com

In memory of my father, Big Paul, who left us in June of 2002, before the championship season, but cheered on the Buckeyes from a far better place.

"Till you're better paid, Chief!"

CONTENTS

ACKNOWLEDGMENTS

*H*aving the chance to be involved in such an exciting field does not come without help and support from many. Ever since 1998, it's been my pleasure to serve as the play-by-play announcer for the Ohio State Radio Network. There are so many who work very hard but get very little acknowledgement for their efforts, and without them, it would not be possible for a single word to be broadcast about Buckeye football or basketball, and I would be lost without them. It is here that I tip my cap to D.R. Railsback, Skip Mosic, Jason Knapp, Bob Taylor, Ted Holbrook, Lisa Alessandro, Eric Kaelin, and Ron McGrew. In particular, a special thanks to the two people responsible for my hiring at Radiohio, Inc., vice president and general manager Dave Van Stone and former executive producer of the Ohio State Radio Network, Ed Douglas.

It's also important to mention the three on-air partners I'm fortunate to have in broadcasting Buckeye games; Jim Karsatos and Jim Lachey for football and Ron Stokes for basketball. You can't help but learn more about the Buckeye tradition by being around such great ambassadors of the school's athletic department, as well as such wonderful people. When each of these teams enjoy success, it's a thrill to see the excitement that exists in the eyes of these guys, who've competed and battled for their love of the sport and the university. If we are all guilty by association, that I'm very glad to be guilty of spending time working with these fine gentlemen.

The experience is made that much more wonderful by the great relationship that we enjoy with the Ohio State University athletic department, because of so many wonderful people. But to mention a few, special thanks to Andy Geiger, the director of athletics, Steve Snapp and Dan Wallenberg from sports information, and the numerous coaches of the two sports I'm involved with, most notably, head coaches Jim Tressel and Jim O'Brien.

But lastly, thanks to all of you Buckeye fans. It's your constant interest and undying loyalty that create the need for us to serve as your messengers. And it's also with you in mind that this project exists: to share the excitement and once again tell the story of the 2002 national championship Season for Ohio State. If people had a chance to witness the turnouts of Buckeye fans on road games this year, and especially in Tempe for the Fiesta Bowl, you would come to understand why the Ohio State tradition is so strong. It's because of the loyalty of those who follow the Buckeyes.

FOREWORD

It was with great surprise and astonishment that I was approached about this project to put into written word stories about the great tradition that is Ohio State football and in particular to try to recapture the moments from a magical 2002 season. You must consider that for the past 20 years I've been fortunate enough to have the opportunity to express the excitement of sports through the spoken word, not through print, but it's a challenge that comes with great curiosity and excitement. After all, I've spent many hours being entertained by the written works of some of my own favorite authors...names like Louis L'Amour, Robert Crais, W.E.B. Griffin, Dan Jenkins, Robert B. Parker, John Sanford, and others.

Ever since the 2003 Fiesta Bowl and the amazing double-overtime win over the defending national champion Miami Hurricanes, people ask, "What was the Fiesta Bowl like?" or "How much fun was the season?"

When you consider that very few people could honestly say, even the most optimistic of Buckeye fans, that 2002 would bring a national title to Ohio State, the thrill of seeing this team win 14 games was immense. Especially with the last-minute drama that came with many of these games. You will read about what happened during the games, but also how it affected me, my co-workers, and others who were along for this wild ride with the Buckeyes.

Some of the quotes and material contained in this story come from the tapes of our radio broadcasts of the 2002 season on WBNS AM & FM, as well as from the archives of the *Columbus Dispatch* in covering the 2002 Buckeyes. Taking the time to listen to those games again and read over the accounts made me realize how fortunate we all were to witness the success of a special team during a special season. There are many plays, moments, and people that were all part of the recipe.

It took 34 years for Buckeye fans who enjoyed the success of the 1968 Ohio State national champions to once again feel that excitement. Who knows how long it will be before the Scarlet and Gray once again reach such lofty heights? But everyone will remember the 2002 season for its last-minute heroics, its high tension, and the team that would never give up. Despite the odds, despite the gaining momentum for the opponent, and despite what was at stake, they would never give up!

INTRODUCTION

More years ago than I care to admit to, my love affair with live sporting events on the radio began. My parents insisted that even in the summer months, when school was out, bedtime for my siblings and myself would be the same as it was during the school year. Our joke about it was that we had to be in bed before the streetlights came on. I shared a bedroom with two younger brothers, and back in the mid-1960s, most families like ours had one television in the house, and it was not in the kids' bedroom. Once we were sent off to bed, the only thing we had for any type of entertainment, besides carrying on with one another, was a box-shaped AM clock radio.

It was on that radio that we discovered the magic of following sporting events that you could not see. While we were aware of the sports teams in our city, and the college teams, we had never seen any games in person, and very few at that time on TV. It was during those hot summer nights that we discovered Major League Baseball, and our local team, the

Cincinnati Reds, and how we could follow every pitch, base hit, stolen base, and all of the stories that came through that box by way of the men who told the stories and described the games.

We heard the names and exploits of people like Pete Rose, Tommy Harper, Vada Pinson, Jim Maloney, Leo Cardenas, Lee May, Chico Ruiz, and many others. We heard about the characteristics of Crosley Field, as well as Connie Mack Stadium, Forbes Field, the Astrodome, and Wrigley Field. We learned that the enemy existed in the persons of Cleon Jones, Donn Clendenon, Sandy Koufax, Roberto Clemente, Maury Wills, Willie McCovey, Willie Banks, and countless others.

It wasn't only baseball that became captivating on the radio. At the time, the Cincinnati Royals (now the Sacramento Kings) were playing in the NBA at the Cincinnati Gardens. There were the college teams, like Ohio State, the University of Cincinnati, Miami University, and Xavier University. In times in which you might see one college game per week on TV, every weekend you could follow games on the radio, every play, every Saturday. Listening to these games provided not only entertainment, but needed diversions at times. As a high schooler, I worked as a paper boy, delivering the afternoon editions of the *Cincinnati Post* and *Times Star*. I walked a route that involved delivering more than 200 papers, six days a week. Fall weekdays often were made easier to tolerate by listening to the baseball playoffs and World Series games back when they were all-day games. They were great enjoyment, even if the Reds weren't playing. Saturday afternoons brought about either day baseball games or, in the fall and winters, college football and basketball, and even, at times minor league hockey. The sounds of the games were as good, if not better, than any music that could accompany a person while performing whatever chore.

At this time in a normal kid's life, he would be caught up in playing knothole baseball, street football, and pickup basketball games. Those certainly were things that I had the chance to enjoy, but it became very obvious at an early age that athletics in my life would be only a recreation, and certainly not a vocation. That point was driven home even harder by seeing some of the athletic abilities of my younger brothers and other kids during those formative years.

It was during those years that while all of us idolized the sports stars of the time, I listened to the voices of those men who brought the events of games to us over the airwaves, envied the jobs they had, and enjoyed the moments they presented us with. There were the nightly summertime narrations of Jim McIntyre and Joe Nuxhall, who called the Reds games on the radio, to be followed by the likes of Al Micheals and Marty Brennaman. During the winter nights of the NBA seasons, it was the voice and excitement of Dom Valentino coming from not only the Cincinnati Gardens, but places like the Cow Palace in San Francisco, the Palestra in Philadelphia, and Veterans Coliseum in Phoenix. Through these games on the radio you could follow the exploits of the Cincinnati Royals with players like Sam Lacey, Nate Archibald, and Tom Van Arsdale. College games came over the air with announcers like Marv Homan, Bill Sorrell, and Dave Piontek, covering Ohio State, the University of Cincinnati, and Xavier University, respectively. In later years, with the AFL expansion coming to Cincinnati, it was the radio that brought the voice of Phil Samp describing Paul Brown's Bengals franchise.

It was with the excitement from following these teams and players that it became very much a dream and goal of mine to develop an involvement in sports through broadcasting. Having been thrilled by the excitement of these teams that the broadcasters brought, I hoped to be able to bring that excitement to others. As I continued to chase the dream, and as opportunities eventually came my way, it was also my hope that one year, one season and at least one time, I would be able to broadcast a championship season: to see a team get to the ultimate goal. When I first took the job calling Ohio State games in the summer of 1998, they were the preseason top-ranked team in the nation. Many felt that it was a year in which the Buckeyes would reach the level they hadn't reached since the championship campaign of 1968. A late-season loss to Michigan State ended that dream. Who would have known the chance for a championship experience would come in 2002?

CHAPTER 1

EXPECTATIONS

As is always the case, prior to the start of any season, fans of each particular team across the country begin mulling over, with great emotion, the prospects of their favorite team. When Ohio State fans began pondering what the 2002 campaign might hold for the Buckeyes, they were reflecting back upon a 7-5 season. It had ended with a tight loss to South Carolina in the Outback Bowl, but was highlighted by a surprising victory in Ann Arbor, over archrival Michigan in rather unusual circumstances.

While many expected the Buckeye defense to be strong, there were questions about who would man the two cornerback positions. There were also questions about the offensive line: Who would replace Johnathan Wells and Jamar Martin in the offensive backfield? And despite his stellar performance against Michigan, lots of folks really wondered if Craig Krenzel was the best player for the quarterback position. The kicking game, which was shared by two first-year players the season before, was also a spot of concern. Almost every Buckeye fan, or media person who covered Ohio State, spoke along the lines that if this team was going to have any success in 2002, the defense was going to have to carry much of the load.

Amongst the media people who regularly cover the Ohio State football team and weren't exactly sure what to expect from this team was Marla Ridenour of the *Akron Beacon-Journal*. "I picked them in the top three [media preseason poll] behind Michigan and Iowa. I knew the defense was good and was fired up by the potential of Maurice Clarett, but was uncertain about Krenzel, and the offensive line was a huge question mark." But when trying to think about what would make her optimistic about 2002, she stated, "Even if Clarett wasn't what he was advertised, they should be okay at running backs with Lydell Ross and Maurice Hall, and I knew Tressel would find the best quarterback, but I didn't know if they had one there."

Spring Game...Injuries

The annual rite of spring for Ohio State, their Spring Scrimmage, brought about numerous questions that centered around injuries at key positions. The offensive line was hampered severely, and once the spring game was played, folks from other positions were shifted there in order to get through the routine. Incoming freshman tailback Maurice Clarett, who graduated high school early to get a jump on his collegiate career, was unable to play because of a hand injury. All-America linebacker Matt Wilhelm, lineman Shane Olivea, and others were absent from the spring game while recuperating from previous injuries. Also, some of the offensive work was limited with only two scholarship quarterbacks in camp. These limitations added to some of the cautious optimism surrounding the Buckeyes heading into the 2002 season.

The quarterback position, as always, brought lots of questions.

Who Will Be the Quarterback?

As is always the case with any football team, the quarterback position gets almost as much, if not more attention, than any other position on the roster. Going into 2002, there still existed questions about who would play quarterback for Ohio State.

Fourth-year junior Craig Krenzel, from Utica, Michigan, had the most experience heading into the season, with junior Scott Mc Mullen from Grandville, Ohio, the only other scholarship signal caller on the roster at springtime. The lack of another scholarship quarterback was the result of Rick McFadden transferring following the previous season. Following their redshirt freshman seasons, both Krenzel and McMullen spent their time serving as understudies to Steve Bellasari and getting very little playing time. For a couple of years you could refer to them as 2-A and 2-B, and occasionally they'd get a little mop-up duty.

McMullen made quite a splash the very first time he stepped onto the field. It was on the final play of the opening game of the 2002 season against Fresno State, a game punctuated by four defensive touchdowns. After Bellasari and Krenzel had each taken some snaps behind center, McMullen came out and had one offensive snap with seconds left on the clock, just after the Bulldogs had just scored. With that one play in the final seconds, McMullen hit wide receiver Ricky Bryant in the end zone, and it left folks wondering what the future might hold for this young man, who set numerous high school records at Granville.

Krenzel, at that point, had not really done anything to distinguish himself to the layperson. But the two second-string quarterbacks had very little opportunity to show their mettle, since OSU rarely enjoyed large enough leads to get them significant playing time. There were times when Buckeye fans were unhappy with the play of Bellasari behind center, but Jim Tressel stood his ground with the senior, explaining that he had always had great faith in having seniors on the field.

Things changed drastically, however, at the tail end of the 2001 season when Bellasari was suspended days before the Buckeyes' home finale against Illinois, following a legal issue. After bearing the brunt of much second-guessing by Buckeye fans, this unfortunate incident came when Bellasari was playing perhaps some of the best football he had enjoyed while a Buckeye. This put Jim Tressel in a very tough position, and he appointed Scott McMullen as the starter for the Illini game, with Krenzel as backup, hoping his quarterbacks and his team would rally around one another and do what was needed while Ohio State was still a factor in the conference race. But Ohio State was handed their second straight loss at home to Illinois, despite the inspired play of tailback Johnathan Wells. The senior tailback wore Bellasari's number eight on his wristbands, as a tribute to his suspended teammate.

Following that game, head coach Jim Tressel announced that Bellasari's suspension would continue into the traditional season-ending clash with archrival Michigan. Craig Krenzel was given the starting assignment against the Wolverines in Ann Arbor, in a game that still had implications on the Big Ten title. As Krenzel prepared for this gigantic challenge in his home state, you couldn't help but think back to earlier in the season, when he wasn't even in attendance on an October game day.

When Ohio State's scheduled game with San Diego State was postponed due to the tragedy of September 11, 2001, rescheduling was an easy task, since both schools had the same October open date. However, it became a problem for Craig Krenzel, because his sister had planned her wedding well in advance on what was originally the Buckeyes' open Saturday. The coaching staff allowed Krenzel to miss the game with the Aztecs due to these unusual circumstances, a decision maybe made a little easier by the fact that Krenzel had not even seen game action to that point in the season. And along with Bellasari, there were two other scholarship signal-callers on the squad, Scott McMullen and Rick McFadden (prior to his decision to transfer to Akron). At that time no one could have imagined that a young man with an excused absence would one month later be starting the biggest game of the season.

With concern heavy about Ohio State's hopes of tackling a Michigan team still hunting for a share of the conference title, and nightmares of previous disappointments against the Wolverines, the Buckeyes surprised all by ambushing the Maize and Blue in their own Big House, jumping out to a quick three-touchdown lead. Yes Johnathan Wells rushed for three first-half scores, and 100 yards before half. And yes the Scarlet and Gray defense harassed Michigan into multiple turnovers. But it was the calm, cool, mature performance of Krenzel behind center that helped Ohio State punctuate its 2001 season with a win in Michigan Stadium.

But despite Craig Krenzel's performance in the Michigan game, questions still existed about who would quarterback the Buckeyes in 2002. Skeptics barked that Krenzel might have been a one-game "flash in the pan," while Buckeye fans from the days of the "three yards and a cloud of dust" offensive school reveled in the way that Krenzel operated a low-risk but highly efficient game plan that emphasized the run and called on the pass when needed. Also, much of the quarterback question had little to do with anything Krenzel did or did not do, but with who was coming into the program.

Freshmen to the Rescue

While college football recruiting and the announcements by high school players of their signing-day decisions have gotten more and more attention over the years, the recruitment of quarterback Justin Zwick from Massillon Washington High School in Ohio and the anticipation of his decision of which school to attend reached epic proportions. Zwick had shattered just about every imaginable high school passing record in the state of Ohio during his time both at Massillon Washington and Orrville High School. Many felt that he was the biggest quarterback prospect in the state of Ohio since former Buckeye signal caller Art Schlichter turned heads at Miami Trace High School.

Buckeye faithful drooled over the prospect of Zwick committing to Ohio State and hoped the fact that his older brother, who had played for Jim Tressel at Youngstown State, would be a key element in the young man's choice.

Ironically, the announcement from Zwick that he would attend Ohio State came while most of the sports focus in central Ohio was on Tiger Woods's quest to win his second straight Memorial Golf Tournament at Murifield in Dublin, Ohio. Once Zwick made his verbal commitment in the spring of 2001, many felt he would arrive in Columbus poised to grab the starting quarterback spot in 2002. Some of these feelings, understand, were fueled by criticism of Steve Bellasari's play at that position during the 2001 season and Krenzel and McMullen being somewhat unknown commodities.

Following all of the hype surrounding his recruitment, Justin Zwick continued to be the main focus of the incoming group of freshmen. I can recall people phoning sports talk shows predicting that the freshman would eventually become the starting signal caller in 2002, and many of these predictions came before Zwick had even signed his letter of intent. You couldn't help but hope this wouldn't create undue pressure on a young man with great promise.

A hand injury during summer drills briefly halted Zwick's progress, and as the season opener with Texas Tech drew closer, all of the talk about the quarterback positon in Ohio State's summer camp surrounded Craig Krenzel, with Scott McMullen at No. 2 and with Zwick and fellow freshman QB Troy Smith pulling scout-team duty, and headed for redshirt status.

Media Day Prognostications

As almost a rite of summer, the Big Ten conference holds their annual media day sessions in Chicago, signaling the approach of each college football season. From a working standpoint, it provides opportunities for media representatives in Big Ten regions the chance to gather info on all 11 teams. This would include information about the personnel, hopes, and expectations for all of the big ten teams.

Each year, many of the media that plan on attending submit their preseason selections for offensive and defensive Conference Players of the Year, as well as a predicted order of finish for the top three teams. The pollsters selected Lloyd Carr's Michigan Wolverines as the choice to win the league title, followed by Ohio State, with Michigan State a third-place selection. While wide receiver Charles Rodgers of Michigan State was selected as the preseason Offensive Player of the Year, the Buckeyes were represented by senior safety Micheal Doss as the Defensive preseason honoree.

The choice of Michigan was based strongly on eight returning starters on defense and 15 starters overall returning from a team that finished a game behind Illinois in the 2001 title chase. Ironically, Ohio State played a large part in thwarting Michigan's championship aspirations. It was the Buckeyes' win over the Wolverines in Ann Arbor, coupled with an Illinois win over Northwestern a few days before on Thanskgiving, that kept Michigan from sharing the league crown with the Illini.

The choice of Ohio State for second was based on the anticipated strength of the defense and the hopes that the offense would find its groove in time.

Michigan State was a team that many expected a great deal from, with 15 returning starters plus the presence of Charles Rodgers at wideout. The Spartans would not appear on Ohio State's 2002 schedule, so there was little thought among Buckeye followers about what would occur in East Lansing. But as the 2002 season played out, Michigan State became probably the biggest disappointment in the league.

Also lost in the preseason hubbub were the Iowa Hawkeyes. Folks figured that the team would be better, as head coach Kirk Ferentz had brought the program along slowly to the point where they had been in the days of Hayden Fry. But no one expected that Iowa would finish the regular season with just one loss and run through Big Ten play unbeaten. Had it not been for an early-season loss to Iowa State, who knows if it would have been Iowa playing for the national championship instead of Ohio State? One thing is for sure: it's a shame that the Hawkeyes and Buckeyes did not get to meet on the field in 2002 to determine a clear-cut winner of the conference. Eventually Iowa and Ohio State would share the Big Ten conference lead, but the Hawkeyes' season would end with a disappointing loss to Southern California in the Orange Bowl.

Off-the-Field Problems

As the start of summer practice moved closer for the Ohio State football team and the anticipation of another year grew stronger, the time leading up to the start of the 2002 season was not without its difficult moments for head coach Jim Tressel.

The 2001 season ended with the first-year head coach dealing with the controversy surrounding his starting quarterback running afoul of the law less than 48 hours before the home finale and having to issue a two-game suspension. Tressel now found himself facing other situations that required tough action. The most notable was that involving linebacker Marco Cooper, who figured to gain substantial playing time in the upcoming year. Following the spring game, Cooper was stopped by police and was found to be in possession of a weapon and illegal narcotics. He was eventually booted off the team.

By the time the season started, Tressel faced other incidents involving other players, was forced to suspend a number of them for the start of the season, including senior wide receiver Chris Vance, who was held out of the first two games.

While most realized the difficulty that a coaching staff faces when dealing with young men of this age group, and in this time when the perils are greater than what many of the coaches or other generations of players experienced, there were questions about whether the Buckeye ship was being run tight enough. It became obvious, as the season moved along, that Jim Tressel and this coaching staff did indeed have a proper handle on how to govern this football team. In this magical season when the players were called upon by the coaches to lay it on the line, they responded as all would have hoped and made coaches, fans, and followers all proud of the mettle these young men showed in crucial situations.

Four-Headed Tailback

As summer practice began in late July for Ohio State, among the positions that observers were watching with great anticipation was that of tailback. Freshman Maurice Clarret's hand injury in the spring delayed the unveiling of the highly regarded ball carrier, and all were anxious to see if the buildup was legit. His size alone grabbed your attention while watching him perform the simplest of drills in practice. As mentioned before, he graduated early from Harding High School in Warren, Ohio, hoping to take advantage of the extra time with the football program regarding weight training and conditioning, as well as getting a jump on the academic adjustment.

The returning group of tailbacks included sophomore Lydell Ross, who ran as first backup to Johnathan Wells the previous season. Ross had shown some impressive flashes with a two-touchdown, 100-yard performance against Indiana and some elusiveness in the Buckeyes' night win over Northwestern in the Horseshoe. It was thought by some that Ross might be considered a slight front-runner based on just experience alone.

The other two participants were sophomore Maurice Hall and redshirt freshman Ja Ja Riley. Hall had been used in small doses as a freshman, mostly in kick return situations, and had been highlighted as a slotback, who was handed the ball while moving in motion. A local product from Columbus, Hall's calling card was his speed.

Riley had been recruited from San Diego, California, and was redshirted in the 2001 season with the surplus of backs at that position. Unfortunately for Riley, his summer drills were interrupted by an appendectomy that cost him practice time and saw him fall behind the other three in the pecking order. The 2002 season provided very little playing time for Riley, prompting his decision to leave Ohio State and transfer closer to home.

Not only was the coaching staff addressing the tailback position, but they also faced the task of replacing Jamar Martin at fullback. He was considered by many to be one of the best to ever play that position at Ohio State and had gained employment, to no one's surprise, in the National Football League.

A curveball was thrown into the works when Jessie Kline decided to give up football. Having grown up in the shadows of Ohio Stadium, and starring at Upper Arlington High School, Kline had moved between the two running back spots, but also fought numerous injuries. This was a young man whom the coaches said was held in very high regard by his teammates, and when he announced his decision to leave the team just days before the season opener, it caught everyone off guard. This also caused some immediate questions at fullback due to the opening-game suspension of Brandon Joe.

Freshman Speaks Out

Not only was Maurice Clarett gaining attention for his ability and his performance on the practice field, but he was gaining it in a way that many would have preferred that he didn't. In the week leading up the Ohio State's season opener against Texas Tech, Clarett stunned those following the Scarlet and Gray by telling reporters he didn't think the team was working as hard as they should have been during one of the practices. Former players were shocked that someone who hadn't even put on a uniform and played a single down would make such remarks, and there was concern about how the upperclassmen on this team would react to such criticism from one of their own.

As the season went on, head coach Jim Tressel often spoke of the great work ethic that Maurice Clarett exhibited, and this incident may have been an offshoot of his burning desire. As the week came to a close, all eventually saw that this isolated incident had no apparent ill effect on the team, but it did result in more limited media access to Clarett.

Red Raiders and Heisman Hype

It's not terribly unusual that in a week leading up to a football game you hear lots of talk regarding the upcoming Ohio State opponent, their strengths, their past accomplishments, and their better players. As the 2002 season opener crept closer for the Buckeyes, much was being bandied about regarding their opponent for the Pigskin Classic at Ohio Stadium, the Texas Tech Red Raiders. Much of the pregame build-up surrounded their quarterback, Kliff Kingsburry, who had already set numerous school records in the passing department heading into his senior season.

Part of the mystique was a clash of styles that many anticipated, as well as a meeting of teams from two of the conferences that got lots of preseason hype. Texas Tech was coming to Columbus billed as another of those "basketball on grass"-type offensive attacks, squaring off against what most figured would be a dose of old-fashioned Big Ten running football. And while there is a certain Midwestern prejudice that the Big Ten has been, is and always will be among the power brokers in college football, many considered the Big Twelve to be among the top conferences, with their highly regarded members, Oklahoma, Nebraska, Texas, and Colorado, getting most of the acclaim. It was still unknown whether Texas Tech and others absorbed in the merger of the old Big Eight and Southwest Conferences were up to the same standard of some of those considered the more traditional powers in that league.

Added to the pregame build-up was that some of the Red Raider players said they thought Ohio State would be an average team in the Big 12. Also, consider that oddsmakers had installed the home team as only a six-point betting favorite, and numerous pundits were speculating on a possible Red Raider upset in the Horseshoe. These were just a few more ingredients that began fueling a season-long fire in the 2002 Ohio State Buckeyes.

Ohio State coach Jim Tressel watches from the sidelines during the third quarter of the Buckeyes' 45-21 victory over Texas Tech. Behind Tressel are Michael Jenkins (12), Steven Moore (3), Lydell Ross (30) and Maurice Hall (28).

Reaching Back for Inspiration

One of Jim Tressel's high priorities when he became head coach at Ohio State was to bring the present-day players closer to the past traditions that have made generations of Buckeye fans so passionate. The first sign in this effort was during spring drills in 2001, when the number of former players attending practice was noticeably higher. Plus, former players were given preference in viewing accessibility on the practice fields. As it turned out, this was just a small start.

The next step was Coach Tressel inviting former team captains to speak to the team prior to the start of games, both at home and on the road. The pregame deliberations were not limited to football, but the messages had definite connections. As Ohio State was ready to take the field against Texas Tech in the 2002 opener, the invitation was extended to, and accepted by former Team Captain Chuck Csuri. His legacy is one that surpasses first downs, yards per carry, and forcing opponents to punt. Csuri gave up his senior season of college football in 1944 to play in a much greater game, against a far deadlier opponent than this year's players would face. Csuri was just one of a number of Buckeyes who surrendered the sport to defend the honor of their nation in World War II.

"He challenged them to be focused and disciplined," said head coach Jim Tressel after the game's conclusion.

"He's an extraordinary person. You could hear a pin drop in the room when he was talking," said Tressel. "Our guys really stopped and listened, because I thought they did a good job of that today."

Whether it was Csuri's presence, the jet fuel provided by the comments of the Texas Tech players, or simply that Ohio State's players were anxious for the season to start, all components played a part of what would turn out to be a memorable liftoff for the 2002 campaign.

CHAPTER 2

KICKOFF!

For those who've never attended an Ohio State home game, it is very hard to describe the setting of the campus area and the tailgating that goes on during game days, and do it justice. Recreational vehicles show up on Friday afternoons, if not sooner, in the parking lots around the stadium. Scarlet and Gray flags are displayed atop vehicles, barbeque grills, coolers, tables, and lawn chairs, and of course the sounds of "The Best Damn Band in the Land" coming from portable music sources are all part of setting the mood. Combine this with the anticipation that's built up within Buckeye fans through the winter, spring, and summer months, and you maybe get a little bit of an idea why a home opener brings about a high level of excitement.

Once the game with Texas Tech began at Ohio Stadium on August 24, it was very obvious to Buckeye fans in attendance, and to the national TV audience viewing the tilt, that this young freshman running back from Warren, Ohio that everyone had been buzzing about was all that and a bag of chips! Maurice Clarett made everyone forget about his midweek criticism of his teammates by tearing loose with 175 yards, three touchdowns, and an average of over eight yards per carry.

A 59-yard scoring run in the first quarter by Clarett was just an appetizer! The youngster then scored on jaunts of 45 yards and one yard in the third quarter to go along with two other rushing scores turned in by sophomore Tailback Lydell Ross. The end result was a 45-21 win for 13th-ranked Ohio State. The rushing explosion by Clarett overshadowed the season-opening performance of junior quarterback Craig Krenzel, who was 11-14 passing and rambled for 34 yards himself.

The Ohio State defense was what many were banking on as the solid part of this team coming into the season, and they did nothing to lessen those expectations. They held the Red Raiders to 66 yards rushing. The aforementioned Heisman Hopeful, Kliff Kingsbury, passed for 341 yards and three TDs, but much of that damage came after the game was well in the Buckeyes' hands. The Buckeye defense also came up with a Dustin Fox interception of Kingsbury, seven quarterback sacks, and nine tackles for loss. "This is definitely a statement game," said middle linebacker Matt Wilhelm. "From the get-go to the end of the game to the singing with the band, this is what you're going to see week in and week out." But there was no question the day belonged to Clarett, who became the first true frosh to start at tailback for Ohio State in a season opener since 1943.

In-State Matchup

A number of years ago, Ohio State made the commitment to play in-state schools, with a large majority of these games to occur in Ohio Stadium. Some of the thought was to keep the money made by the opponents within Ohio's boundaries as opposed to letting the dollars go to out-of-state opponents. Also, it was thought that fans of those schools within the state would jump at the chance to purchase tickets for games in Columbus and that it would provide a thrill of a lifetime for those players of the other teams who were not fortunate enough to play for the Buckeyes.

The plan, however, had come close to backfiring on more than one occasion. Teams like Bowling Green, Cincinnati, Ohio University, and Miami of Ohio had all taken turns providing big scares to Ohio State in recent seasons. But through it all, the Buckeyes managed to prevail. The 2002 season brought about a meeting with Kent State, which had seen some resurgence in its program under head coach Dean Pees.

While the Buckeyes' offense kicked it into high gear, posting its second straight game with 40 or more points, the defense flexed some of its anticipated muscle. Senior safety Michael Doss and freshman linebacker A.J. Hawk returned interceptions for scores. It was Doss's fourth career score but his first on an interception return. For Hawk, it brought more attention to the group of freshman linebackers that followers were hearing about. Hawk, from Centerville High School in Dayton, had been lauded for his football instinct and his intensity. Along with fellow linebackers Mike D'Andrea from Avon Lake, Ohio, and Bobby Carpenter from Lancaster, Ohio,

Ohio State quarterback Craig Krenzel applauds his team's performance against Kent State.

there were young pupils that brought about great optimism for the future of the Buckeye defense.

Senior safety Donnie Nickey attributed a lot of the success to the team's overall focus.

"There's been less of the little things that distract other players in the locker room during the preperation for the game."

En route to posting a 51-17 win over the Golden Flash, Craig Krenzel continued to show his efficiency behind center, completing his first 11 passes (12-14 with 190 yards and a TD pass), but he was bent on improving.

"Today we'll take a couple of hours off, relax, and then I'll start watching some film. And starting tomorrow evening, it becomes, 'What do we need to do to be successful this Saturday?' And I think if the team can keep that attitude, it doesn't matter who you're playing. We're going to be a good football team."

Clarett continued his impressive first year with two scores, one on the ground and one by catch. Maurice Hall scored his first career OSU touchdown.

Another sign of good things to come was the performance of sophomore kicker Mike Nugent, from Centerville. In 2001, Nugent went through what maybe could be called freshman inconsistency, but year number two was a gigantic step forward. In a season that would conclude with a handful of school records and All-America honors, Nugent booted three field goals, all 40 yards or longer, against Kent State.

The win over Kent State continued to stoke enthusiasm for Buckeye fans about this year's team, but all were anxious to see how this unit would fare in their next encounter against a ranked Washington State team.

Heisman Hype Part II

If Buckeye fans thought they had gotten a serious dose of buildup for a possible Heisman Trophy candidate in week one with Kliff Kingsburry of Texas Tech, the second helping would be healthy as well, with Washington State and Jason Gesser coming to town for game number three.

Gesser, a senior QB for the Cougars, had and would set numerous passing records at a school that had produced the likes of Jack Thompson, Timm Rossenbach, Drew Bledsoe, and Ryan Leaf. Also, Washington State was the preseason pick of many to win the Pac-12 title, and there was a lot of talk about the game between the Cougars and Buckeyes being a possible preview of the Rose Bowl or better.

While Gesser's Heisman candidacy was the center of much pregame chatter, it was once again Ohio State's freshman Tailback Maurice Clarett who stole the show. His 230 yards on the ground was the sixth best single-game total in Ohio State history and the second best ever for a freshman (second to Archie Griffin's 239 in 1972 against North Carolina).

"Everybody kept talking about getting respect back for the program," said Clarett.

"I think in the second half we showed that we were the better team." Clarett found the end zone twice, and coupled with three more field goals of 40 yards or better from Mike Nugent and a team safety, Ohio State delivered a convincing win to their fans, to a national TV audience, and to those who maybe had doubted their first two conquests. The Buck-

Ohio State tailback Lydell Ross (30) runs from Washington State defenders Jason David (29) and Virgil Williams (24) in the second quarter of Ohio State's 25-7 victory over the Cougars.

eyes dispatched Washington State 25-7 and threw a monkey wrench into the Heisman hopes of Jason Gesser, sacking him twice and forcing him to throw two interceptions as Ohio State improved to 3-0 with a 25-7 win.

As Clarett continued to be the focus of everyone's attention, the efficiency of quarterback Craig Krenzel was once again under-noticed, but that was mostly because he wasn't needed in a large manner. Krenzel finished the game throwing only 10 passes, and completing four of them. Also lost in the final score was the fact that the Buckeyes had to come from behind, trailing 7-6 at half, but the defense showed what would be a season long trend, staying tough in the second half, keeping Washington State from scoring again. Head coach Jim Tressel said, "We wanted our defense just to keep coming at 'em, coming at 'em, coming at 'em."

Now unbeaten in their first three games, with two of them against teams ranked in the top 15, confidence was high about Ohio State, who at the time was ranked sixth in the nation, but which was also preparing for its first game away from home.

Clarett's Injury

During the football season, head coach Jim Tressel and selected Ohio State football players are made available to members of the media who cover the team every Tuesday at noon in the Buckeye Hall of Fame Cafe, a sports-themed restaurant near the campus. It's similar to what goes on with most any of the major college football programs, where info is gathered by radio, TV, and print reporters on not only the just-completed game for Ohio State, but on the upcoming opponent. On the Tuesday following the Washington State game, most of those in attendance were in for quite a surprise.

As was Coach Tressel's usual routine, his comments first covered the just-completed game, then moved on to the upcoming game. Following his review of the win over Washington State, Tressel surprised all by revealing that Maurice Clarett had suffered a knee injury against the Cougars and that the freshman running back had undergone arthroscopic surgery and would miss the fourth game of the year in Cincinnati.

The good news was that it appeared his time on the sideline would be limited to just the one game.

Probably even more stunning was how Tressel shared this revelation, indicating that Clarett's injury was a known occurrence. I can remember every media person in attendance exchanging looks of surprise, for Clarett's injury was unknown at that time to anyone outside the football program. This injury ended up being the lead story for every media outlet covering the Buckeyes. I clearly recall leaving the room to call our radio station on my cell phone to get this information on the air as soon as possible. The response from the person who fielded my call was something like, "Are you kidding me?"

I can also remember one day before this announcement, talking on the phone with a friend of mine in Cincinnati, who was a Bearcat fan and planned on attending this game. This person joked that they hoped Clarret wouldn't get 300 yards against UC. They wouldn't have to worry about that now.

Bearcat Scare!

It was the first time in 91 years that the Buckeyes were the visiting team in Cincinnati. To say it was a festive atmosphere when Ohio State traveled south to play the Bearcats of the University of Cincinnati was like saying grass is green. These two teams would play in Paul Brown Stadium, named after the former Buckeye head coach who led Ohio State to its final national title in 1942. The facility was named after Brown for his efforts to bring an expansion American Football Leauge Franchise to the Queen City in the late 1960s.

It was also the final homestand for the Cincinnati Reds baseball team in Riverfront-Cinergy Field and the weekend for the annual OktoberFest, paying tribute to the strong German heritage in the River City. The weekend got off to an ominous start when the Reds game that Friday night with Philadelphia was rained out, prompting the scheduling of a day-night doubleheader for Saturday, with the Buckeyes-Bearcats game set to kickoff at 3:30 p.m. It had the possible makings of a real snarl in a downtown area already besieged by massive construction.

From a personal standpoint, this game, much like when the two schools played in 1999, would be different from any other Ohio State game. I had spent nearly a decade broadcasting games for the University of Cincinnati before being offered the job in Columbus to call Buckeye games. There are many wonderful people at UC who have great meaning to me for the time I spent with them. Among those people is Rick Minter, the Bearcats' head coach. Just a few months earlier, Rick had gone out of his way to phone me and express his condolences over the death of my father. The hard work of Rick, his players and coaches over the years had taken the Bearcat program from one of the worst in the nation to one that their fans could be proud of. One of the greatest memories I have of my days calling games for Cincinnati was seeing them end the longest postseason streak of any 1-A program in the country in 1996 and beat Utah State in the first ever Humanitarian Bowl in Boise, Idaho.

There were other people, like my former radio partners, Jim Kelly and Scott Springer, and university staffers like Tom Hathaway, Brian Mc Cann, and athletic director Bob Goin, who had been very good to me for years. And it was great to see all of these folks in what would be a wonderful football setting.

But make no mistake about who I wanted to win this game. Despite the special things that had happened in the past with my association with the University of Cincinnati, business concerns came first, and it was my hope, like it is every Saturday, that Ohio State would finish on top. I can only imagine it's similar to what athletes go through when they face a team they had previously played for.

Prior to this game, Ohio State head coach Jim Tressel wondered if this would be the first serious adversity his team would encounter and how they would handle it. Many players from both teams were involved in the 1999 game in Columbus, in which the Buckeyes had to rally from behind to secure a win over UC. The more than 66,000 who jammed into PBS, the largest crowd ever to witness a sporting event in the city's history, were in for high drama.

Cincinnati set the early tone and at halftime enjoyed a slim 12-7 lead. It was a first-half performance that left Buckeye supporters shaking their heads. The only Ohio State score prior to halftime was a Krenzel TD pass to tight end Ben Hartsock. Former Ohio State All-America offensive lineman Jim Lachey, who serves as color commentator for the Ohio State radio network, commented on the absence of Maurice Clarett and said, "You would hope that one 18-year-old doesn't make this much of a difference."

The worm began turning in Ohio State's favor in the second half. Craig Krenzel hooked up with Chris Vance on a TD pass in the third quarter, and defensive end Darrion Scott

Ohio State safety Will Allen (26) intercepts a pass intended for Cincinnati receiver LaDaris Vann in the end zone to clinch a 23-19 win for the Buckeyes over the Bearcats.

turned in one of the big hits of the season, separating the football from Bearcat quaterback Gino Guidugli. That fumble was receovered by tackle David Thompson, who said, "It looked like a million dollars laying there, so I jumped on it." Crag Krenzel's spinning, twisting and swirling six-yard touchdown run with a little more than three and a half minutes to play ended up being the decisive score, but it wasn't the end of the excitement.

The host Bearcats, sights set on what would undoubtedly have been one of the biggest wins in the program's history, began a final drive from their own 20-yard line to the Ohio State 20 with a little more than a minute to play. Guidugli then had four cracks at the needed touchdown. His first-down pass into the end zone was dropped, and the second-down throw was incomplete. On third down it looked for just a quick second like UC had grabbed the upset. Backup QB-wide receiver Geogre Murray was on the receiving end of a Guidugli pass, and it appeared he had come up with a catch that would have those dressed in Black and Red ready to erupt! Instead the ball slipped through Murray's hands, giving life back to Ohio State. Following a timeout, Guidugli, on fourth down and with 32 seconds left, tossed a pass down the middle of the field, headed toward the end zone. But before a Bearcat could have a chance at making a catch, Buckeye middle linebacker Matt Wilhelm was able to get a mitt on the ball, misdirecting it from intended receiver LaDaris Vann and allowing safety Will Allen to come up with a game-saving interception in the end zone. Twenty six seconds later, the Buckeyes left Paul Brown Stadium with a 23-19 win in a game that had been in doubt all day.

To a man, the Ohio State players realized they had dodged a bullet. Senior safety Mike Doss said, "We came out and got lucky, a little bit lucky!" Jim Tressel also summed up the feelings of everyone connected with Ohio State on that day against Cincinnati.

"We're very fortunate to leave Paul Brown Stadium with a win, but I'm awfully proud of the way our players kept playing and playing. That made the differnce."

There were some notable results from that Buckeye win on the riverfront. Sophmore tailback Lydell Ross, carrying the load in the absence of Clarett, rushed for a career-high 130 yards on 23 carries. Ross had been the player most affected regarding lost playing time due to Clarett's success. It was after the Cincinnati game that another Columbus radio station very irresponsibly ran reports that Ross was unhappy over his lack of playing time, and wanted to transfer to Florida State. It was a rumor that Ross himself quickly denied.

The Cincinnati game also featured the debut of wide receiver Chris Gamble as a defensive back. In the 2001 season, the coaches had toyed with using Gamble in certain situations if need be on the back line. While that had never occurred, there was a feeling his call on defense might come against Cincinnati's multiple-receiver alignment. In our radio broadcast booth at Paul Brown Stadium prior to the opening kickoff, we were in fact told by Ohio State's director of sports information, Steve Snapp, that Gamble had been used in practice as a defensive back during the week, but we were asked not to use that information unless Gamble did in fact enter the game on defense. That way if he was not called upon, the information was still quiet. Gamble's second-half pick of the

UC quarterback was part of a stretch in which Ohio State forced the Bearcats to turn the ball over the last three times they had possession.

The Scarlet and Gray had managed to compile a 4-0 record against non-conference teams, and were headed home to their friendly confines of their massive Horseshoe to begin play in the Big Ten Conference.

Ohio State coach Jim Tressel and the team sing the school's alma mater, "Carmen Ohio" after defeating Indiana 45-17 in their Big Ten opener.

CHAPTER 3
THE BIG TEN

Conference Opener

While all Buckeye fans were breathing a collective sigh a relief following the escape from Cincinnati, it was time for the focus to shift for at least one week to the Big Ten Conference. The Buckeyes would open league play at home against Indiana, team that hadn't enjoyed a win at the expense of OSU dating all the way back to 1987. It was also the anticipated return of Maurice Clarett and the curiosity regarding how well his knee had healed following a one-week absence. This would also be a gander at the league's lone new coach for 2002, Gerry Di Nardo, who had enjoyed success at Vanderbilt and LSU.

For those asking the question about Clarett's ability to pick up where he left off, the answer came in the form of a three-touchdown, 21-carry, 100-plus-yard outing as the Buckeyes secured a 45-17 win over IU. Senior linebacker Cie Grant dubbed the freshman running back "Maurice the Beast!" "I think Maurice is developing a reputation. He runs hard, and anyone at the game knows this guy runs harder than any freshman I've ever seen!"

Clarett did have to receive medical attention in the second half and have the stitches in his right knee re-done, but he returned to the game. According to Clarett, "I try to be one of the toughest people on the team, because people winning games have to be tough."

While Clarett's return was up to his early standards, others played a large role in getting league play off on the right foot. Kicker Mike Nugent booted a career-long 51-yard field goal. Dustin Fox blocked a punt that set up another score. And Chris Gamble scored his first Ohio State touchdown, taking it to the house on a 43-yard reverse from his wide receiver positon. Now at 5-0, and 1-0 in the conference, head Coach Jim Tressel tempered his review of the day's success. "I think we're a better team than we were a week ago, but we're not where we want to be."

After the game, when asked what he told his team following the defeat, Indiana coach Gerry DiNardo said, "I want the buses quiet!"

Under the Light and In the Air

Week number six of the 2002 season brought about what many looked at as Ohio State's first "real" road game, an evening encounter against Northwestern in Evanston, Illinois. This would be the Buckeyes' first appearance in Ryan Field since they were the number-one team in the nation in the fall of 1998. Even though they had played in Cincinnati two weeks ago, many considered this the Buckeyes' first true test away from home, since a majority of those watching the UC-OSU game at Paul Brown Stadium were clad in Scarlet and Gray.

There were other unusual twists to this game. The Big Ten Conference and their agreement with EPSN put this game into the evening hours for prime-time viewing. I can tell you from personal discussions with members of Ohio State's Athletic department that they are not fans of night games. I'm certain that much of it is a feeling shared by many longtime Ohio State and Big Ten fans in general, that football is best meant to be played on Saturday afternoons. But TV, and its accompanying revenue, makes it hard for schools to hold on to some traditions. It seems that in recent years, Ohio State has played an average of one night game per season. There are some faithfuls who will tell you they enjoy the evening games because of the additonal hours it allows for tailgating. But in many cases, it seems, those are the folks who aren't always the best judges of what's going on by the time kickoff occurs.

As freshman tailback Maurice Clarett continued to be noticed for his play on the field, his fear of flying was revealed when the Buckeyes traveled by air for the first time in 2002. Exactly when this fear originated, and exactly how it was dealt with, did not become public information. Bottom line, he arrived in Evanston and experienced some real ups and downs all in one night.

The upside for Clarett, he rushed for two touchdowns, surpassed 100 yards on the ground, and turned in his fourth 100-yard game in the four he dressed for. The downside for the freshman: he lost three fumbles and had a sideline spat with his position coach, Tim Spencer, captured by the TV cameras. But when the smoke cleared, Ohio State had finished on top with a 27-16 win.

Aside from the freshman's dramatic night, Ohio State found itself trailing Northwestern after one period by a 6-0 score. The Wildcats had to settle for field goals twice when drives ended inside the Buckeye 10-yard line and eventually missed on two other kicks for three points.

Once again lost in the other segments of this game was the performance of quarterback Craig Krenzel. He rushed for 62 yards of his own and passed for 170 yards. End result: the Buckeyes' 23rd consecutive win over Northwestern and their first 6-0 start since 1998. But as the team headed home, the Clarett controversy would once again dominate discussions leading into the next week's game.

There was also the revelation that some in the Ohio State traveling party might have had a hard time sleeping the night before the game. There was apparently some sort of dog show in the Evanston area that same weekend, and some of the owners and their canine contestants were in the same hotel. Woof! Woof!

Do You Know the Way Back to San Jose?

It might seem odd that Ohio State would come back home and play a non-conference game on October 12, but in fact it was the second year in a row for such an occurrence. In 2001, the Buckeyes found themselves hosting San Diego State at midseason, but that game had been rescheduled following the cancellation of all division one games after the September 11 terrorist attacks. This season's game with San Jose State was to be Ohio State's homecomming game, which brought up a sore subject in its own right. The Buckeys had lost their last two homecoming games.

The Spartans of San Jose State had wreaked havoc in Big Ten territory earlier in the season, scoring a win at Illinois. They came to Columbus leading the nation in takeaways, but the Buckeyes fed their opponents a little of their own medicine, forcing and recovering four fumbles and coaxing the visiting quarterback to throw one interception. Defense was certainly at high alert in Ohio State's 50-7 win over San Jose State.

The Spartans were going to do all they could to strike through the air, foregoing any serious rushing threat. Although Scott Rislov set a school record with completions and completion percentage (36-44, 265 yards and one TD), he was harrassed by the Buckeye defense all day. Linebackers Matt Wilhelm and Cie Grant turned in solid hits, and Grant in particular had one collision with Rislov that resulted in a fumble, recovered by Mike Kudla. Grant was pleasantly surprised at his clear path to the quarterback. "I came through so clean and I thought, 'Oh man, he doesn't see me coming.' My whole intention was to punish him."

While the defense was up to snuff, the offense was not to be outshone. Quarterback Craig Krenzel passed for over 240 yards and hit three diffrerent receivers, Maurice Clarett, Micheal Jenkins, and Chris Vance, on scoring strikes. "A lot of that stemmed from the time I had," said Krenzel. "O-line

Ohio State's Darrion Scott (56) and Simon Fraser (75) celebrate after a third-quarter fumble recovery. The Buckeyes beat the Spartans, 50-7.

did a great job, and whenever you don't get touched back there, it's pretty easy to go through your progressions and make big plays."

Clarett, by the way, had another 100-yard day on the ground and a pair of scoring jaunts. The Ohio State offense, in fact, scored five of the first six times they had the ball in the second half. And kicker Mike Nugent booted three field goals, tying the school record of 15 in a row held by Vlade Janikievski. That streak for Nugent dated back to the season finale of 2001 in Ohio State's win over Michigan in Ann Arbor. All was right in the Scarlet and Gray universe, but right around the corner loomed another stiff road challenge.

The Great Logo Caper

Now that the Ohio State Buckeyes had reached the 7-0 plateau, they moved up to number four in the national poll and were no longer under the radar. But at this point of the season, all were waiting to see if this team could do what others in the recent past couldn't: take steps farther along the chain to greater goals.

The coaches and players alike knew that crunch time had arrived. Senior safety Donnie Nickey said, "We've been successful so far, but we know that the next six games is were we do our job, where our work has to be done. This is the meat. This is what we came to Ohio State to play for."

The next week of the season would provide the toughest test this team had seen so far, at least from a phsyical stand-point, against the Wisconson Badgers, in rowdy, raucus Camp Randall Stadium. Head coach Jim Tressel went about preparing his team, mentally, for the increased challenege. "Obviously we know the road ahead of us, beginning with the Badgers at Camp Randall, but I think our guys are anxious to step up and see how we fit into the whole picture."

While the Badgers had been one of the more dominant teams in the conference in recent years, they had been struggling. Wisconsin had dropped seven of its last nine home confrence games going into this tilt. They were minus Lee Evans, considered one of the leauge's top recievers, who broke his leg during the Badgers' spring game. Two years previously, Ohio State scored a win in Madison sparked by an early-game 80-yard touchdown run by Derek Combs. Wisconsin, in each of their previous two visits to Columbus, overcame double-digit deficits to score wins in the Horseshoe.

One of the subplots to the Wisconsin-Ohio State series was the "Great Logo Caper." Since the road teams had been enjoying the success, each school's recent wins had included players from the victorious squads dancing on the defeated team's center-field logo, drawing the ire of the losing school.

Another additional element was controversy surrounding a photograph of Wisconsin's quarterback Brooks Bollinger from the Badgers' win in Columbus the previous year and his signature of that photo that allegedly insinuated that Wisconsin owned the Horseshoe. It made for a great buildup to what turned out to be a fantastic game.

From a personal standpoint, I always look forward to when Ohio State plays Wisconsin, whether it's in Madison or Columbus and whether it's football or basketball. It gives me a chance to rub elbows and talk shop (among other topics), with one of my favorite colleagues, Matt Lepay, the Badgers' radio play-by-play announcer. I jokingly refer to Matt as "Mr. Bad Influence." That's because of some of the late night-early morning sessions we've enjoyed discussing sports, broadcasting, cigars, or any of the other numerous topics that come up when we put our heads together. To be fair to Matt, we each are guilty of "influencing" the other. It's been fun when I've had the chance to gather with Matt, and his wife Linda, when the Buckeyes and Badgers meet and usually at the Big Ten basketball tournament. One year we even ended up on vacation at the same place, at the same time, completely unplanned! Both Matt and his wife are native Ohioans, so that always makes for some common ground.

What really gets the fur flying is when we can combine Iowa announcer Gary Dolphin into a quorum with Matt and me. It can get really deep at those select times. Usually when two of the three have gathered, it involves late-night phone calls to the third missing party to report in on the evening's events.

The Buckeyes struck first with Craig Krenzel hitting Micheal Jenkins in the first quarter with a 47-yard TD pass, and it was not the last time these two would connect for a big play in Camp Randall Satdium in this day. By halftime, the Badgers had gained the upper hand, owning a 14-10 lead. Ironically, Brooks Bollinger, the Badgers' signal caller, was knocked out of the game with a concussion right before half, and Jim Sorgi seemed to ingite the home team, delivering a scoring pass to Johnathan Orr.

The third quarter was a stalemate, but in the fourth, Craig Krenzel again went to work. When facing a crucial third and six from the Ohio State 16, Krenzel airmailed a pass that

Micheal Jenkins outjumped two defenders to haul in, giving the Buckeyes a much-needed first down and keeping the drive alive. The decisive score came when Krenzel found tight end Ben Hartsock on a three-yard TD pass.

As Jim Sorgi marched the Badgers downfield and threatened Ohio State's lead and perfect season, Sorgi went for the kill, chucking the ball into the end zone for Johnathan Orr. Two-way player Chris Gamble, back in at defensive back, picked off the pass and preserved another win in tight circumstances.

The Buckeyes survived with a 19-14 come-from-behind win at Wisconsin, and one of the true team leaders set one of the biggest examples. Senior safety Mike Doss finished with 14 tackles and talked about the team playing with heart and winning with guts. "I think it shows our desire, to keep winning, to keep plugging at it." Doss was also proud of being able to contribute with his play. "As we football players like to say, we've got to eat every week. I had to eat today, I had to step up to the challenge."

Other key performances: Tailback Maurice Clarett, who turned in a 133-yard rushing day on 30 carries. Then there was Punter Andy Groom, who, late in the contest when a drive stalled for Ohio State, delivered a huge, 74-yard punt that landed in Wisconsin's end zone, giving the Buckeye defense room to operate.

Here Comes Penn State

Confidence was extremely high the following week when Ohio State came home with an 8-0 record, 3-0 in the Big Ten, and still ranked fourth in the nation. The Buckeyes were to host Penn State, and there's always a bigger lift in people's steps around the campus on a football Saturday when the Nittany Lions or the Wolverines from Michigan come to town.

The game also marked the return of Adam Taliferro to Ohio Stadium. Two seasons earlier, as a freshman defensive back, Taliferro suffered neck and spinal injuries late in an Ohio State win over Penn State. The injury occurred when Taliferro was tackling Buckeye running back Jerry Westbrooks and lowered his head into the ball carrier.

On that day two years previous, the Ohio Stadium crowd was silent for many moments while trainers and doctors attended to the fallen football player. After he had been taken to the OSU Medical Center, there was immediate concern about whether Taliferro would even walk again, let alone compete in this sport. Among the many who spent time looking in on the injured Penn State player during his convalescence in Columbus were former Ohio State head coach John Cooper and a number of the Buckeye players. No longer playing football, Taliferro accompanied the Penn State team to Columbus and was introduced to the crowd at the stadium and greeted with music, applause, and affection. Throughout the entire ordeal, Adam Taliferro and his family expressed their gratitude to the many at Ohio State and in Columbus who showed concern for him.

Ohio State's Chris Gamble (7) runs to the end zone past cheering teammates for a touchdown after intercepting a Penn State pass in the third quarter of the Buckeyes' 13-7 victory.

The next few hours brought about different feelings. The encounter between the Buckeyes and Nittany Lions in the Horseshoe was more like a prison riot. The game was as physical as could be expected. As you would imagine, many of the Ohio State players were asked if they felt a need for atonement following a loss one year ago at Penn State in which their Buckeyes let a 20-point lead get away. While the success of the Scarlet and Gray had gotten a great deal of the pregame billing, Penn State tailback Larry Johnson was turning many heads himself. Johnson, just a week previous, had gashed Northwestern for 257 yards and presented a big-league challenge to the Buckeye defenders.

On Ohio State's first possession, things seemed to be rolling along nicely until quarterback Craig Krenzel fumbled the ball at the Penn State one-yard line. For a few scary seconds from the radio booth high atop Ohio Stadium, it looked like Anwar Phillips was going to take the football all the way the other way and give their visiting team a giant shot in the arm. But in what set the foundation for this day's script, wide receiver Chris Gamble showed great fortitude in tackling Phillips 58 yards farther downfield. Gamble was the first two-way starter in many years for Ohio State, getting the opening call in this game on both sides of the line of scrimmage and totaling more than 100 plays, including special teams.

Offensive success for either team was hard to come by. Penn State owned a 7-3 halftime lead. Quarterback Zack Mills triggered many crucial plays in Penn State's come-from-behind win over the Buckeyes in Happy Valley the year before, but was experiencing firsthand what others had felt all season long: the intense pressure applied by Ohio State's defense. As the left-hander tried to find a receiver downfield in the third quarter, Chris Gamble once again came to the rescue. The sophomore from Sunrise, Florida, stepped in front of a Mills pass and raced 40 yards to the house, giving the Buckeyes the big play they needed to deflate the Nittany Lion surge. It was the third pick of Mills on the day, and from there it was cruise control for the Buckeyes, who finished the day with a 13-7 win. Gamble's assessment of the big play: "I saw the ball, I attacked it!"

"They met a defense that was on a mission," said head coach Jim Tressel. The Scarlet and Gray defense held Penn State to 179 total yards of offense, only 81 on the ground. And Larry Johnson was limited to 66 yards rushing on 16 carries. And on a day of simple statements, legendary Penn State coach Joe Paterno explained, "We couldn't make a play when we had to."

One significant play early in the day sidelined Maurice Clarett not only for the day, but for much of the next few weeks. After turning in a 30-yard rush that allowed Clarett to surpass the 1,000-yard rushing mark, the star freshman left the game with a shoulder "stinger" that would become the most discussed injury in Columbus for weeks.

Also notable about this day, in which Ohio State improved to 9-0 overall and 4-0 in the Big Ten, was that the crowd was certainly at peak performance. It's hard to imagine more than 100,000 people in one stadium not being loud, but at times you do hear folks talk about how the crowd sometimes gets settled in and comfy. At one point in the second half of this tight game, my partner in the radio booth, Jim Lachey nudged me to take the headphones off and listen to the noise. It's something that we don't usually take the time to notice, but on this day it was worth noticing. Loud only begins to describe it!

Remember the Gophers

The start of November found Ohio State playing their final home game until the season-ending clash with Michigan. Their opponent, the Minnesota Golden Gophers, were coached by former Buckeye player and assistant coach Glenn Mason. It was just two years before that Mason had brought his team to Columbus, waxed nostalgic about his days at OSU as the team bus drove down High Street, and then watched his ball club feed off his emotion and upset the Buckeyes. That was Minnesota's first win at Ohio State since the 1940s!

While all were singing the praises of Ohio State's defensive successes, there was anticipation of their collision with the Minnesota offense that averaged over 270 yards rushing per game, and two running backs, Terry Jackson II and Thomas Tapeh, who each had run for more than 100 yards in their three previous games.

Things started well for the visitors on this day. A blocked punt set up a Gopher field goal that gave them an early 3-0 lead, but that would be the last time they visited the scoreboard. With the shoulder stinger sidelining Clarett, Lydell Ross rushed for two TDs and gained 89 yards. Maurice Hall, used very sparingly on scrimmage plays since his fumble at Cincinnati, added 93 more on the ground, including the game's final score. Add to that another outstanding defensive outing, and the Buckeyes had reached ten wins alongside no blemishes after downing Minnesota 34-3.

Ohio State quarterback Craig Krenzel (16) looks downfield for a receiver in the first quarter against Minnesota. Krenzel had nine completions for 128 yards in the Buckeyes' 34-3 defeat of Minnesota.

Defensive lineman Darrion Scott had two sacks, and cohort David Thompson had two tackles for loss. Donnie Nickey blocked a Minnesota punt. On the other side of the ball, Craig Krenzel found Chris Vance on a 30-yard scoring strike. And kicker Mike Nugent booted two field goals to set a school record with 20 in a row during the 2002 season, 21 straight overall. Also adding to the defensive job turned in by the Buckeyes against the Gophers, OSU yielded only 112 yards of offense, just 53 on the ground. The Buckeye defense also extended a streak of ten straight quarters without allowing a touchdown. While Ohio State's offense was outscoring their opponent 17-0 in the third quarter, the Gophers were only able to run 13 plays during that span, netting a minus six yards and failing to gain a first down.

Now that the offense seemed to have regained some of its stroke, they still paid homage to their defensive brethren. Quarterback Craig Krenzel stated, "They've carried us the past two weeks. The offense came out a little slow again today and the defense kept us in the game." Krenzel and wide receiver Micheal Jenkins continued to operate on their own solid frequency. Midway through the second quarter, Krenzel found Jenkins on a key 49-yard catch and run that ended up at the Gopher five-yard line and set up the two rushing touchdowns by Ross.

While Ohio State kept dreams of an unbeaten season alive on that day, the company at the top got a little smaller, thanks to Notre Dame falling to defeat for the first time that season, losing to Florida State. Now 10-0, the Buckeyes would wander away from home for two weeks, hoping to avoid land mines on the trail.

Tragedy Strikes

Nothing prepares any of us for death. As the 2002 football season was rolling along wonderfully for Ohio State, and as the Buckeyes were preparing for the game against Minnesota, tragedy struck. Not once, but twice!

Junior defensive end Will Smith learned that one of his friends had been killed in a shooting in his hometown of Utica, New York. His week was interrupted by a trip home to pay his final respects.

Then senior wide receiver Chris Vance learned on the morning of the Minnesota game that his brother had been shot to death the night before in Ft. Myers, Florida. Vance received the news by way of a voicemail from his mother. Vance relayed that he had spoken with his brother earlier on that fateful Friday and that they pretty much spoke on a daily basis.

Now this young man had to face one of the most difficult moments in life while he was supposed to be getting ready to play a football game. "I think it was important that I play," said Vance. " I wanted to play because I knew he wanted me to play. We were real close, and it was just something I knew he wanted me to do." Vance also seemed to figure out pretty quick that any immediate source of strength was going to come from his teammates.

One of those Vance leaned on was quarterback Craig Krenzel, whom he had roomed with the night before the game. End result: Vance used his game-day assignment to begin his own mourning process and surround himself with what occupied his everyday life.

Prior to kickoff, we were informed in our radio booth about the tragic shooting death and that Vance would dress and play. We were asked by university officials not to mention anything about the incident on the air, because it wasn't known how much had been done regarding proper notification. Then in the fourth quarter, when Vance caught a 30-yard touchdown pass from Krenzel, he dropped to his knees and pointed to the heavens, a gesture that needed no explanation.

Shortly after that play we were informed that the announcers on ABC televison had explained the story about Vance's brother having been tragically killed. So the door was open for us to inform those listening about Vance's tragedy, and to express our own condolences.

While Chris Vance did play in that Minnesota game after learning of his brother's death, he did miss the Buckeyes' next game at Purdue to attend the funeral. Also, during the week leading up to the Minnesota game a season earlier, Vance experienced the death of his father. He managed to play in that game against the Gophers also. You can't help but feel for a young man who at a young age has had to endure two great losses.

Home Stretch

With a 10-0 record and with wins having been impressive, but nothing close to easy, Ohio State was now getting deeper into the meat of their schedule. All along, folks looked at the final three weeks with trepidation: back-to-back road games at Purdue and Illinois, and then the home finale against

Michigan, who has broken so many dreams before. This was where you had to figure the Buckeyes would take their biggest steps toward a conference title, then perhaps bigger achievements such as a BCS bowl bid or a chance to play in the national championship game.

Week number eleven found Ohio State preparing to play a Purdue team that wasn't widely considered a threat on paper to derail the Buckeye express. But this was a Boilermaker team, and in particular an offensive attack, that the OSU coaches had a great deal of respect for. Joe Tiller's Purdue offense had become known as one of the many "Basketball on Grass" teams with their multiple wide receivers and downfield passing attack. The Boilers were not the offensive threat they were in the days when Drew Brees was playing quarterback, but they still had serious talent on offense, and it had become obvious that Tiller was trying, over the last few years, to get the defense on pace with what they had achieved offensively.

As Ohio State prepared for this game at Ross-Ade Stadium, it seemed like it wasn't that long ago that Purdue beat the Buckeyes en route to winning the Big Ten title in 2000. It was a back-and-forth battle, and Ohio State seemed to have gained some late momentum when Mike Doss intercepted Drew Brees, and Jerry Westbrooks powered his way to a fourth-quarter rushing touchdown. But Brees used a deep TD pass to Seth Morrales to give the Boilermakers the lead for good. The Buckeyes' last effort to come from behind died when a snap from center to quarterback out of a shotgun formation hit a motioning receiver, resulting in a fumble recovered by Purdue and sealing their biggest win in years.

Going into this game in West Lafayette, Indiana, many Ohio State fans who were not fortunate enough to have tickets for the home finale against Michigan started making plans to take in the final two road games, hoping to glimpse what all thought could be a special run at the end of the year. Even prior to kickoff at Purdue, Scarlet and Gray-clad OSU fans were in strong appearance. The stands were ringing with the chants "O-H" and "I-O" long before kickoff.

The early portion of the game belonged to both teams' defense. Purdue got on the board first thanks to a field goal with less than a minute to play in the first quarter. It looked like that would be all of the offense prior to halftime. Just before the break, Buckeye quarterback Craig Krenzel had two key rushing plays to get Ohio State in position to kick a tying field goal right before the half. And when I say "right before" the half, the score occurred with time speeding off the clock.

Following a run by Krenzel, Mike Nugent and the field goal unit hurried on to set up for the kick for three points. Players on both teams were scrambling to get into position, and once Nugent banged the 22-yarder through the uprights, there were some tense moments while the officials were put on the spot to determine whether or not the kick was good. To the dismay of the Purdue players, coaches and fans, and to the relief of the Buckeyes, the kick was ruled a successful one, and Ohio State gained a measure of momentum heading into the break with the game tied at 3-3.

Once the second half started, the defensive struggle continued, or maybe it's better stated that the offensive struggles continued. Purdue got 100-yard passing performances from both of their quarterbacks, Kyle Orton and Brandon Kirsch,

Ohio State's Michael Jenkins, right, catches a 37-yard touchdown pass from quarterback Craig Krenzel over Purdue's Antwaun Rogers. The Buckeyes defeated Purdue 10-6.

but couldn't find the end zone. For that matter, they really couldn't muster a running game, either. The Ohio State offense ran into similar difficulty. Tailback Maurice Clarett was still hampered by his lingering shoulder stinger and gained little more than 50 yards on 14 carries.

Things got scary in the fourth quarter when Kirsch connected on a long pass play with Ray Williams of over 50 yards, but Donnie Nickey was able to haul down Williams, and a subsequent Matt Wilhelm sack of the quarterback forced Purdue to settle for a another field goal. But they owned a 6-3 lead with a little less than eight minutes to play, putting the onus back on the struggling Buckeye offense. The struggle got even more difficult when the OSU drive went bust, prompting Andy Groom to punt away. Groom put Purdue back at their own eight-yard line, and the defense, leaned on all day, answered the challenge again and held the Boilers to a three-and-out.

This set the tone that would seem to be the standard for the rest of the season. After Chris Gamble's punt return that put the ball at the Purdue 46-yard line, the offense looked for the spark that had eluded them all day. Consider again that the Buckeyes were minus the rushing threat of Clarett, or any others for that matter. Purdue's defense came into this game bent on stopping the run, and forcing Ohio State to beat them through the air, and that's what occurred in the final three-plus minutes. A third-down pass from Craig Krenzel to tight end Ben Hartsock left the Buckeyes one yard short on fourth down from the Purdue 37-yard line with a minute and a half to play.

The stage was set for the most memorable play of the season to date. It would also be one of the most memorable plays of Ohio State's charmed season. Only one yard was needed to keep the drive going, but yards on the ground were being guarded like gold by the Boilermakers. When the ball was snapped, and when Craig Krenzel dropped back to pass on fourth and one, it had to have initially caught many by surprise that Ohio State, known for three-yards-and-a-cloud-of-dust, would try to get this job done in the air. Even more nerve-wracking, Krenzel was dancing in the backfield to elude the pressure, and then it even seemed like he stumbled a bit before letting loose with the pass. Once the ball was in the air, if you weren't already holding your breath, you did so then, knowing that everything hinged on the success of that pass.

Meanwhile, on the other end of the play, Micheal Jenkins was jockeying for position to catch the pass. He was motoring down the left sideline, and defensive back Antwaun Rogers was jostling with Jenkins to try to either break up the pass or pick it off. Using his size and locking in on the ball, Jenkins outfought the defender, made the catch, and despite the coming pass interference penalty, carried the ball into the end zone for the biggest completion and six points of the season. On a day in which the offensive success had been kept in check for the most part, the Krenzel-to-Jenkins connection began a stretch that would be big for Ohio State in the tightest of situations and would continue to be as the march to a championship continued. Jenkins's catch from Krenzel and the point after gave Ohio State a 10-6 win over Purdue, and for the first time in Buckeye football history, Ohio State was 11-0!

I wouldn't have remembered the line right away, but after having heard it replayed by our radio station a few times, I was reminded of the comments I made on the air right after the Krenzel-to-Jenkins touchdown pass secured the win for the Buckeyes. I said, "Ohio State has found a little magic that has eluded them all day," in reference to coming up with a big offensive play when the offense had struggled all day.

The Buckeye defense again threw a blanket over their opponents: They had now put together a stretch of 12 straight quarters without allowing a touchdown (dating back to the Wisconsin game). They picked off Purdue's quarterbacks three times, one of them a Dustin Fox theft in the end zone early in the game, and a diving pick by Matt Wilhelm to kill a Purdue drive. Wilhelm also had a key sack in the game and seemed to be fueled by the fact that his collegiate career was coming to a close. "Obviously, as a senior, I want to step up," said Wilhelm. "Like Coach Tressel says, 'Play your career best year, and you're going to have the type of season we're having.'" The senior from Elyria Catholic High School showed great promise as a sophomore, then battled injuries his junior year. There was no doubt that he would have to be a vital part of any defensive success Ohio State would have in 2002. Wilhelm's play on that day in West Lafayette, Indiana drew praise from his position coach, Mark Snyder. "What Matt has been doing all year is play the game in his head before it's ever been played. He studies the game."

Another very obvious key factor in this day, as well as all season was the play and leadership of senior safety Mike Doss. In that Purdue game two years ago that we talked about, it was Doss who got beat by Seth Morrales in the game-winning play for the Boilermakers. But on this day, Doss got to enjoy the moment on the same field where he'd endured one of his most disappointing times as a player. "We weren't thinking about two years ago," said Doss. "We've got guys working hard week in and week out. It's a 60-minute game, we kept fighting, we got some breaks near the end."

Eleven down, two to go!

Another One Falls

The Ohio State win at Purdue was thrilling in its own right. What happened in the few hours following that game added to the excitement. It's with this in mind that I will now explain a little of what happens with our radio broadcasting crew once a road game is over.

First off, when Ohio State plays a road game, and especially a conference game, our group travels the day of the game and returns the same evening by charter flight. Our group includes seven people: me, analysts Jim Lachey and Jim Karsatos, our producer, Skip Mosic, engineer Jason Knapp, statistician D.R. Railsback, and Greg Snapp, who handles the parabolic microphone on the sideline. The charter flight includes many more than just our seven. Our radio stations, WBNS AM and FM, are owned by the Dispatch Broadcast Group, which includes the Columbus CBS television affiliate, WBNS Channel 10, and the *Columbus Dispatch* newspaper. The charter flight includes personnel from all three entities that travel for an Ohio State road game.

It's essential to point this out, because once any road game is done and we have finished our radio postgame shows, we are not able to leave until the newspaper writers have finished their stories. While that is an inconvenience to us, it conversely is an inconvenience to the scribes to have to leave as early as we do in the morning of a game because of our needs. So when the Purdue-Ohio State game was over, we had a few hours to kill while waiting for departure.

Usually in this situation, we try to find someplace were we can grab something to eat, maybe enjoy a few adult beverages, and wind down. It helps if we can find someplace to watch some of the other college football games being played. On that Saturday, the game of major concern was top-ranked Oklahoma playing at Texas A&M. Prior to the start of play that day, the Sooners, Ohio State, and Miami (Florida) were the only unbeaten teams left in 1-A football. It was widely believed, fairly or not, that if those three teams finished the year unbeaten, Ohio State might be the team left out of the BCS title game. That certainly is one of the failings in the BCS system, deciding on two of three or more perfect teams for their one championship matchup. Ohio State fell victim to that in the first year of the BCS in 1998. The Buckeyes were preseason number one in the nation, and held the top spot until a November loss in Columbus to Michigan State. Once the regular season ended, and Tennessee was the only unbeaten in the land, the BCS choose a one-loss Florida State team to meet the Volunteers. The Seminoles' defeat had come earlier in the year. The Buckeyes finished that one-loss season with a win over Texas A&M in the Cotton Bowl. So understandably, Buckeye fans had little faith that the BCS would grant Ohio State's wish if they weren't one of no more than two unbeaten teams.

Anyway, our group of seven settled into a little establishment that we found not far from the West Lafayette airport and also not far from Ross-Ade Stadium. Numerous Buckeye fans traveled to Purdue for this game, and they were in high spirits following Ohio State's win. Like those already seated at this establishment, our group set about trying to kill a few hours before our charter flight was to leave.

Following a balanced meal that involved chicken wings and pizza, we raised a toast to the Buckeyes' victory that day, and to witnessing history as Ohio State reached 11-0 for the first time ever! On the TV screens in this establishment, we saw that whatever Big Ten game that was being shown (I honestly can't remember what game it was), the network had given up on the lopsided affair and switched to the Oklahoma-Texas A&M game in College Station, Texas, where the top-ranked Sooners were in trouble.

It seemed that the entire establishment shifted its attention to this upset in the making. We watched the final quarter of this game unfold, and Oklahoma was unable to hold off the Aggies. Texas A&M had upset the Sooners, doing Ohio State a large favor. This left the Buckeyes and the defending national champion Miami Hurricanes as the nation's only unbeatens. The task was simple for OSU: win at Illinois and defeat Michigan in Columbus, and not only was a share of the Big Ten title theirs for the taking, but a shot at a national championship was within reach. All of this just hours after the Buckeyes were a fourth and one away from seeing it all slip away at the hands of Purdue.

Skepticism

Even though Ohio State was 11-0 and, along with Miami, one of just two unbeatens in 1-A college football, there were still doubting Thomases about this team's stature and shot at a national title. It was regarded by Buckeye fans as a lack of respect for their football team, even though they were going into the Illinois game ranked number two in the nation. While Ohio State glided under the national radar early in the season with others among the unblemished, you would have thought some of this would have subsided, especially this late in the season. Quite honestly, I think most people realized if they just kept winning, things would take care of themselves. That's the approach the football team was taking.

In the week leading up to Ohio State's game with Illinois, I received a phone call from a producer of a sports talk show on a Chicago radio station. My name had been passed along by Raymont Harris, a former Ohio State star running back who spent a majority of his NFL career with the Chicago Bears. Raymont was involved in doing Bears pregame shows for this station, and was also doing work for our radio station in Columbus. Getting these kinds of calls is not an unusual thing, but the comments made by this producer (who was also hosting the show I would appear on) typified some of the skepticism about this team.

Before settling on a time and day for the interview, the gentleman said to me, "Do they really expect to win a national title with that offense?" It was the tone of the question that caught me off guard, almost like Ohio State was insulting the football gods with the way they played. Again, keep in mind this was following the win over Purdue, so it was understood why people wouldn't look at the Buckeye offense in the same way that they might look at, say, Miami. But it still struck me odd that a guy who was trying to get me to do something for him would come off so arrogant about a team that was 11-0.

Nonetheless, I did the interview the night before the game. That part went fine, and the guy I had talked with earlier in the week, who had such strong comments about the Buckeye offense, was okay. After all, it wasn't the most un-usual talk show interview I had done. Just the year before I did an interview for a Virginia station during the basketball season where the host didn't know that, number one, the Big Ten had actually started playing a conference postseason bas-ketball tournament, and number two, he thought Iowa State was in the Big Ten and didn't know that Penn State was in the league.

But once the Ohio State-Illinois game was over, I couldn't help but think back to this guy's skepticism.

Next Stop: Champaign

Now standing as one of the two remaining unbeaten teams left in college football, Ohio State prepared for its final road game of the 2002 season, against the team that delivered the knockout blow to the Buckeyes' conference title chances a year before. The Buckeyes would face an Illinois team that had been playing their best football of the season, winning three of their last four, after losing five of their first six games.

One of the lowest points for the Illini was a home-field loss to San Jose State, the same San Jose State team that OSU drilled 50-7 earlier in the year. Illinois also needed a win to keep its chances for bowl eligibility alive. And while the Illini were playing at home, prior to the start of the contest it appeared that Ohio State might have the home-field advantage. Just like the week before, Buckeye fans jumped at the chance to purchase tickets for the game, and there was much Scarlet and Gray in the stands at Memorial Stadium.

The status of running back Maurice Clarett was also in doubt for this game. It's safe to say the freshman from Warren, Ohio, had the most talked-about shoulder in the state, with the stinger he suffered in the Penn State game. While the doctors had given Clarett medical clearance to play, the coaching staff made the decision to keep him on the sideline for this game.

The script didn't seem to have changed much through the first half of the game. Ohio State got a pair of field goals from Mike Nugent, and Illinois got a three-pointer of their own. One of the early Ohio State drives stalled when Craig Krenzel tried to rush into the end zone for a TD, but was ruled to have run out of bounds before reaching the goal line. Penalties on successive plays then pushed the Buckeyes backwards, and they had to settle for three when they were so close to six.

Following halftime, when Ohio State was up 6-3, the Illinois offense found its stride. Jon Beutjer had battled with Dustin Ward early in the season to handle the quarterback position. Once Illinois coach Ron Turner decided to stick with Beutjer, a transfer from Iowa, things started clicking. The Illini

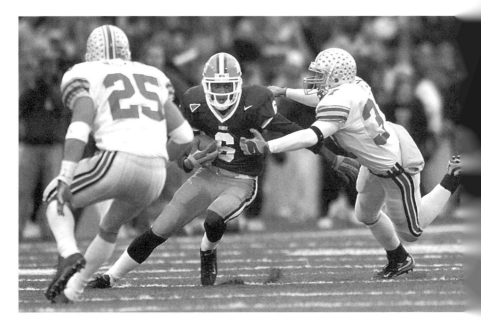

Illinois receiver Brandon Lloyd (6) tries to gain some yards in the second quarter against Ohio St. defenders Donnie Nickey (25) and Dustin Fox (37).

also had three outstanding pass catching threats in Brandon Lloyd, Walter Young, and Aaron Morehead. During the second half, Beutjer started finding his receivers with regularity and eventually hit Walter Young on a 19-yard TD heave. That gave Illinois a 10-6 lead.

Following that strike by the Illini, the Buckeyes' offense again showed some life. The rushing yards were hard to come by, but Craig Krenzel once again turned to his money receiver. Following two rushing plays and an incompletion, Krenzel pulled the trigger and went 50 yards to Michael Jenkins for six points. The junior from Tampa, Florida, outfought defensive back Micheal Hall, who was eventually called for pass interference. The Krenzel-to-Jenkins connection had once again paid off, and Ohio State was on top 13-10.

All season long, part of what helped Ohio State avoid trouble was the play of eventual All-America kicker Mike Nugent. The sophomore had set numerous school records to this point, including consecutive field goals. While he hit three field goals on this day, his streak of 23 in a row came to an end with a first-half 37-yard miss, and he eventually missed another from 41 yards out. Illinois managed to tie the game by the end of the third quarter, 13 all, when they received a 47-yard field goal from John Gockman, one of two kickers Ron Turner had been using during the year. Mike Nugent was not finished, however, connecting on a fourth-quarter 37-yarder that at the time put the Buckeyes up 16-13. All that was needed was for the defense to remain strong and for the offense, once they got the ball, to secure a first down or two.

The Ohio State offense found themselves once again struggling to make things happen. Nugent's second field goal miss gave Illinois possession of the ball with five and a half minutes left in the game. But their drive stalled, and John Gockman missed on an improbable 59-yard try, giving the Buckeyes the ball with 2:17 left.

But the Buckeye offense continued to run into problems and could not secure a necessary first down. With a little more than a minute to play in the fourth quarter, Jim Tressel called on his punter, Andy Groom, and called on his defense to stand tall. From there, Illinois appeared to be the team chasing big dreams. Beutjer led his ball club on drive that moved from their own 25-yard line to the Ohio State 31. Included in that drive was a key fourth-down pass to Greg Lewis. But the clock was becoming a major player in this drama. It was moving too fast for Illinois and not fast enough for OSU.

With just seconds to play, Ron Turner once again called on his kicker, John Gockman, who moments ago had missed on a 59-yard desperation try. At the time, there was very little information on Gockman. It was later learned that he had at one time been on the football team at Iowa. It was after this game in a discussion with Iowa's radio play-by-play announcer, Gary Dolphin, that I learned that Gockman had briefly been part of that program. Gary also said that in a conversation he had with Hawkeye coach Kirk Ferentz, the coach couldn't remember Gockman having been involved with their team.

So the stage was set for Gockman, as it had been set for Ohio State's Dan Stultz two years previous. In that 2000 season, Stultz delivered a field goal in the final seconds of play from 47 yards out (matching his uniform number) to give the Buckeyes a win. Just like Stultz, Gockman connected, but from 48 yards out, and tied the game at 16 all, sending it to overtime!

Overtime! New Territory

For the first time in Ohio State football history, the Buckeyes were playing in overtime. Divison 1-A installed overtime for football ties for the 1996 season. Prior to '96 it had been in place for bowl games. Following the first year of OT, an addendum to the rule was put in place. Starting in 1997, once a game moved into a third overtime, following touchdowns, teams were required to attempt a two-point conversion rather than kick for one point. There was concern in the first year of overtime with the length of some games.

During all this time, the Buckeyes had managed to avoid playing in the extra session. After its inception in '96, there were a few times when we thought it was going to occur, like in 1999 against Purdue, but the Buckeyes blocked a late field goal to secure a win. There was also the Outback Bowl, following the 2001 season, when South Carolina hit a last-second field goal, winning the game and avoiding overtime.

I had joked with my partners about how exciting overtime games were. During the time in which I had broadcast football games for the University of Cincinnati, I had the chance to call three such games, one of them a triple overtime thriller that the Bearcats won over their archrival, Miami of Ohio. From time to time in the booth we would talk about the procedures for OT, just to be ready for it. Maybe a week or two prior to this Illinois game, I had noticed a note in the Big Ten weekly release that Ohio State was the only team in the conference who had yet to play in overtime. Here ends the history lesson.

Ohio State had the first possession of overtime. Remember, the offense had been having problems late in regulation, and those problems seemed to follow them into OT. But quarterback Craig Krenzel once again showed his toughness and on third down and ten from the opponent 25-yard line, rushed to move the sticks and keep the drive alive. That set the stage for sophomore tailback Maurice Hall. Following a crushing block from lineman Adrien Clarke, Hall scooted eight yards into the end zone, the final eight yards of his 69-yard game, and that gave Ohio State a 23-16 lead. Remember again that the success of Clarett and the use of Lydell Ross as the number-two tailback seemed to have pushed Maurice Hall way down the pecking order. It seemed that ever since a vicious hit that Hall took in the Cincinnati game from Bearcat Line-backer Jason Hunt, which resulted in a lost fumble, Hall's chances on scrimmage plays had been far and few between. You couldn't help but feel happy for this young man after he got this gigantic score for the Buckeyes.

It was now up to the defense!

Illinois took possession of the ball, and Jon Beutjer went to work trying to score through the air. A pass to Aaron Morehead was caught just out of bounds. Then Walter Young managed to get behind cornerback Chris Gamble in the end zone, and Young found himself looking up at a pass headed his way. For a few scary moments, it appeared once again that the Buckeye bubble was about to burst. While Young went about trying to make a catch and tightrope an out-of-bounds line in the end zone, the officials ruled that Young had bobbled the pass. Result: incompletion and fourth down.

So once again the Buckeye defense faced a tough assign-ment. It was up to these young men who had hauled such a heavy load all season to once again do their part to deny the opponent. To gut out one last pass rush, to stay with receivers one more time, and make what once again would be the big-gest play of the season.

Fourth down, eight yards to go for Illinois, at the Ohio State nine-yard line. The Illini had, at this point, pretty much abandoned the run. As the ball was snapped, Beutjer looked to throw for Aaron Morehead. From the snap of the ball, two Buckeye defenders, linebacker Cie Grant, and defensive tackle Tim Anderson, scratched off the line and stormed after the quarterback in a bull rush. As Beutjer cocked and fired, his pass struck the forearm of Anderson, a junior from Clyde, Ohio. Once the ball hit the ground, the threat was over, and the second-ranked Buckeyes had once again survived the stiffest of tests and escaped Champaign with a 23-16 win in overtime.

After the game, Anderson admitted that he and his teammates weren't going to give up. "The most important thing is the way we hung in there as a team. We could have given up toward the end," said Anderson, but we kept fighting. I think that's the most important thing that came out of today." Anderson then commented on the final play, "I just stuck my arms up and hoped for the best!" It wasn't new territory for Tim Anderson to make big plays late in a season. In the previous year's Buckeye win in Ann Arbor over Michigan, Anderson managed to blitz his way into an interception from Michigan quarterback John Navarre.

You also have to reflect back on the big catch turned in by Micheal Jenkins earlier in the game, a 50-yard TD pass from Craig Krenzel.

"Nobody said it was going to be easy, playing on the road, trying to win a Big Ten championship," stated Jenkins. "We just stuck together and played 60 minutes-65 minutes tonight and were able to pull out wins on the road."

Once the marathon had ended, Ohio State's players were able to share the moment with the many Buckeye fans who had traveled to Champaign and sat in the cold to test their nerves. At 12-0, Ohio State was coming home to play archrival Michigan for a Big Ten title and a trip to college football's national championship game!

You couldn't help but wonder if they could keep playing tight games like this and coming out on top. There would be a couple more opportunities for that question to be both asked and answered.

Having to Share

While the Ohio State camp was elated to have escaped Champaign with a win over Illinois, the Iowa Hawkeyes had concluded their season on the same day with a win in Minneapolis over Minnesota, claiming their rivalry trophy, Floyd of Rosedale. (Floyd is a bronze pig!)

The win gave Iowa at least a share of the Big Ten title. At 11-1 and 8-0 in the conference, the Hawkeyes knew that they would get at least a BCS bowl bid. With their season done, Iowa would sit at home and await the outcome of the Ohio State-Michigan game to see if they would share the title with the Buckeyes or if they could claim the league crown all by themselves if Michigan prevailed.

The Iowa story for 2002 was really an outstanding one. When head coach Kirk Ferentz accepted the position, replacing Hayden Fry, the program had fallen on rough times. Ferentz had been an assistant at Iowa under Fry when times had been better. While the Hawkeyes had taken their lumps, they more than paid people back during this magical season. Unfortunately for Iowa, they had lost an early-season game to Iowa State, and that kept them just out of reach of the goals that Ohio State seemed destined for. Brad Banks, Iowa's quarterback, had become quite a story himself. A junior college transfer, Banks was unstoppable both on the ground and in the air. Both Banks and Ferentz would finish the year gaining much-deserved postseason honors.

The shame of the whole deal is that with the Big Ten's rotating schedule, Ohio State and Iowa did not meet in 2002, the second straight year they'd missed one another. It's safe to say that such a matchup could have been the highlight of the Big Ten's season, and very possibly home field could have been the determining factor.

You might have thought Iowa would want to see Ohio State beat Michigan, claim a share of the league title, and help boost the league's chances of having two teams appear in BCS bowl games. But a Buckeye loss aided Iowa in that they would then be in the midst of a field of one-loss teams hoping for an invite to the national title game.

There was another spicy little item that added to the whole Iowa-Ohio State mystique. ESPN college football analyst Trev Alberts, on numerous occasions, made comments that while paying respect to Ohio State's achievements, he felt Iowa was the best team in the conference. Alberts, a former star player from Nebraska, is a native of the state of Iowa. That completely enraged Buckeye fans. Understandably what upset people was that for all the success Iowa was enjoying, they were not undefeated, as Ohio State was! It made for some fun discussion on the radio sports talk shows in Columbus.

The closing chapter to the Iowa story was that the Hawkeyes' very successful season did land them a BCS Bowl berth. They were assigned to play Southern California and eventual Heisman winner Carson Palmer in the Orange Bowl. Unfortunately, Iowa suffered their second loss of the season in that game.

Michigan Week

What great theatre! What more could a Buckeye fan expect? The storybook 2002 season had brought itself to a point that Scarlet and Gray fans dream about during the summer months when they anticipate another season, having all the marbles on the line against Michigan. Not only the pride of winning that annual season finale, and not only the Big Ten title being up for grabs, but Ohio State had survived where others had failed, and at 12-0, with only one other unbeaten team in the country, a trip to the BCS showcase title game in the Fiesta Bowl January 3 was at stake as the Buckeyes prepared for the Wolverines.

Any Buckeye or Wolverine fan would chime in that the supposed "Ten Year War" between Woody Hayes and Glen "Bo" Schembechler was what put this rivalry in a special place. The success that Woody had at Ohio State goes without saying. But it was one of Woody's disciples, Schembechler, who restored the roar in Ann Arbor. A Barberton, Ohio native, Schembechler not only played for Hayes at Miami of Ohio, but served Woody as an assistant at OSU before becoming head coach and part of Miami's legendary "Cradle of Coaches." It was from Oxford that Michigan athletic director Don Canham plucked Bo away from the then "Redskins" to take over the Michigan hopes. There are those who considered Bo's act sacrilegious. You cannot, however, argue the success he enjoyed in Ann Arbor.

To try to name a few players and a few of the games in this series that make OSU-U of M the special rivalry that it is would be a tough chore. Ranging from the Snow Bowl, to Bo and Woody, and even to the modern day, any person who ever played or coached for one of these schools would tell you that all of these games were played with great respect and great intensity!

As November of 2002 brought these rivals together, many Buckeye fans were reminded of the heartbreak suffered in past falls at the hands of the Maize and Blue. Three times during the 1990s the Buckeyes had dreams of perfection and hopes of a national crown ruined on the final Saturday of the season. The tenure of former Ohio State head coach John Cooper was haunted by only two wins against "The Team from Up North!" The horrors of past missteps on the last week of the season did have some Buckeye fans worried.

Change in Routine

As expected, with everything that was on the line heading into the 2002 Ohio State-Michigan game, the media attention had intensified. There generally is a great deal of national exposure during this week because of the rivalry between these two programs. But the drama of whether or not the Buckeye team, which had made the last few games so thrilling, could pull it off one more week and exorcise the demons of past disappointments made for good fodder.

As mentioned earlier, part of the weekly routine during football season is the Tuesday gathering held by Tressel, with selected players for media availability. It was announced that during the Michigan week, this would the be last chance that any members of the media would have to speak with the players. In years past, there have been similar changes in the rou-

tine like this during the Michigan week, and it led to speculation among those who might take a pessimistic view on things
that approaching this game differently factored into past
stumbles.

But as this change in routine was put into place, you
couldn't help but remember that this same coaching staff gov-
erned over the Michigan week the previous year with success.
That was even when they were dealing with the suspension of
their starting quarterback for that game and getting Craig
Krenzel, a native Michigander, ready for his first career start
against the Wolverines, in Ann Arbor. You also had to consider that these coaches had presided over this team and its
routines all season long in 2002 and things had worked out
well regarding the win and loss column. So you very much
wanted to assume "benefit of the doubt." You also couldn't
help worry, though, with everything on the line.

Tickets, Anyone?

Trying to chase down tickets for the Ohio State-Michigan game any year is always tough. Trying to secure them for
the 2002 game with a national championship berth at stake
was a massive task. The home-stretch run for the Buckeyes
and the excitement created by their nail-biting finishes at
Purdue and Illinois just primed folks who already had seats,
and the search was on for the usually hard-to-come-by tickets. It went without saying that all expected another attendance record at Ohio Stadium to fall. The frantic chase for
tickets to this game began in earnest as soon as the Buckeyes'
win over Illinois was in the books.

"I started getting calls following the Illinois game," said one season ticket holder who wished to remain anonymous. "Then for the rest of the week, I started getting at least three or four calls a day from people asking if I'd sell. After a while I started cutting people off before they could finish, because I didn't want to hear how much they'd pay and how much cash I'd be missing out on."

Another season ticket holder, not wanting to be identified, said he started getting calls about his Michigan tickets following the win over Wisconsin. "People knew I had access, and I was fielding offers back and forth for about a month, and some of the prices were contingent on whether or not Ohio State remained unbeaten." This ticket holder then stated he had whittled his potential customers down to about three or four people by the week of the Michigan game. "I was shocked at what I was being offered and shocked by what I got. The guy who bought them didn't want his wife to know how much he paid for them."

Then there was another anonymous Buckeye fan who had been looking forward all season long to attending the Michigan game. It was one of two games he would get to see all season. Then, sadly, this fan had to surrender his tickets to someone else when he had to make an emergency trip to Florida to visit his critically ill father (who eventually passed away the day after the game). "I knew that I was going to experience something special by attending that game, unlike any other Ohio State game I ever had seen, or maybe ever would see. But there was no question that seeing my father in his final days was more important than any game."

The lucky person who received that man's ticket couldn't believe that this monumental game would be his first ever Ohio State game in person. "While I felt bad for my friend having to miss the game for the reason he had to, it was the thrill of a lifetime to get this chance and to experience all of what happened on that day."

Michigan Week

The buildup all week for the Ohio State-Michigan game was intense and exciting. There were the usual Buckeye flags on cars, on houses, and in business establishments all over town. The places that seemed to be gearing up the most were hotels, restaurants, and establishments known for serving adult beverages in mass quantity.

You may remember the earlier mention of the "Buckeye Hall of Fame Cafe." This would be a massive day for that location. Every year on the Friday morning prior to the Michigan game (home or away), they stage their annual "Beat Michigan Breakfast," opening their doors at 6:00 am. It is a marathon day for the restaurant and its employees. It's also a bonanza day for revenue. For those unfamiliar with it, The Cafe is a combination of sports bar, restaurant, game room, and banquet facility. It's decorated with a very strong Ohio State athletic theme. There are party rooms named after Woody Hayes, Fred Taylor, and Jack Nicklaus. There are stars on one of the hallways with the names of All-Americans from all sports at Ohio State. Even one of Archie Griffin's Heisman Trophies is displayed prominently. Football season is the busiest time of the year for the Buckeye Cafe.

One of my co-workers, Ian Fitzsimmons, from Sports Radio 1460 The Fan, WBNS-AM, was there to host his afternoon talk show from the Buckeye Cafe. "It was an absolute madhouse by the time I got there at 4 p.m. People had been there since 4 a.m.; by the time we went off the air at 7 p.m., the crowd was in a frenzy. It was standing room only!"

While most people were getting full gear into their Friday night mode, the Ohio State basketball team was playing its final exhibition game at the Value City Arena. Ever since that building was open for business, it seems like in most years the Buckeyes have either had an exhibition or a regular-season game on that Friday night before the Michigan contest. This night, the Harlem Globetrotters were the opponents, continuing their trend of playing serious exhibition games against college teams. Even prior to this game, OSU basketball coach Jim O'Brien had stated he felt this could be one of the best teams they would play all season. That changed considerably by the time the game was played. The Globetrotters had changed coaches and had had some personnel changes as well, so things had not gone smoothly. But for Buckeye fans waiting for the following day's clash with Michigan, it was a chance to enjoy a little more of a sporting atmosphere. Usually on these Friday nights before the Michigan game, some Wolverine fans manage to find their way inside the Value City Arena and take a lap around the upper concourse waving a maize and blue flag with the big block "M" on it. It usually serves to fire up OSU fans even more.

One more notable occurrence on this night regarding basketball: The Buckeyes suffered two notable injuries in their win over the Globetrotters. Point guard Brandon Fuss-

Cheatham and power forward Shun Jenkins both were hurt, proving to be key losses for the basketball Buckeyes early in their season.

Following our broadcast of the basketball game, I ventured into the Buckeye Hall of Fame to meet some friends who were coming to Columbus for the next day's football game and were staying at my house. I had also visited the cafe for lunch earlier in the day, so I got a chance to see some of its noon-hour atmosphere. Suffice to say it was party central! It was obvious there were some folks who had been in there most of the day. There was one particular female patron who was not shy at all about showing anyone who cared the block "O" tattoos she had strategically placed on a certain portion of her anatomy. There were others who had come in just to witness those who had been reveling for several hours. You could tell it was special, that you were on the eve of what could be the biggest day experienced by many of these Buckeye football fans to date. The accomplishments of 1968 were just stories to most of these people, and they wanted to soak up as much of 2002 as they could.

As Friday night turned into Saturday morning, you knew it was going to be a chore for many of these people to wake with the clearest of heads, but that they would struggle through whatever was needed to have their best game-day face on.

Game Notes

As the Michigan game got closer, the questions regarding Maurice Clarett's shoulder continued to be asked. All had hoped that his limited play over the last several weeks would be of benefit. Even though Maurice Hall and Lydell Ross had performed admirably in Clarett's absence, Buckeye fans knew that the chances of Ohio State winning were increased with Clarett able to perform as he did early in the season.

There still were questions about the Buckeyes' ability to throw the ball deep and throw it consistently. Craig Krenzel and Michael Jenkins had proved to be a big-money connection late in games, but you wondered if they could hook up more often to avoid late-game heroics. The thought of Chris Gamble and his two-way duty occurred in your mind. In the Illinois game, there were times when the Illini went right after Gamble, as well as Dustin Fox, and had enjoyed some success. Questions had been asked in media circles about weather or not Gamble was starting to feel the physical toll of playing on both offense and defense. It was now common for him to appear in around 100 plays per game. One thing that in this season generally never got questioned much was the Buckeye defense. The only thing that rolled around in your mind after all the bending that they had done was the hope that they wouldn't break in this game. After all, an awful lot had been required of them all season and especially in the recent weeks.

Then there was the yearly question of what new wrinkle might occur in this game. In lots of cases, when Ohio State and Michigan played in the season finale, one team or both would have some new play or new formation that they hadn't used all season. This extends all the way back to the days of Bo and Woody. There were even times back in the days of the "Big Two and Little Eight" (when the league was basically a two-team race between U of M and OSU) that the coaches would install things for Michigan in earlier weeks when they generally felt certain they would have an easy time with other opponents.

Michigan was coming into this game with some things at stake themselves. They were 9-2 on the year, 6-1 in the conference, and winners of three in a row. They were hoping to return the favor of a season before to Ohio State. The Buckeyes' win in Ann Arbor in 2001 allowed Illinois to win the league title. Remember also that the Wolverines had beaten the Buckeyes the last time they visited Ohio Stadium. One person you had to imagine would be anxious for atonement would be Wolverine quarterback John Navarre. He was bounced all around by the Buckeye defense a year before, and at one point in that game was even replaced briefly.

Suffice it to say that as this game day drew nearer, Buckeye fans were anxious for what could the biggest football day of their lives, but nervous about what could possibly be an enormous disappointment if things went badly. No one really wanted to think about that!

Game day

As you would expect on November 23, 2002, it was cold in Columbus. I don't even remember the exact temperature, but it was cold. It's always cold on Ohio State-Michigan day, and you should always be prepared for that. The morning drive from home to Ohio Stadium on a game day is usually a very peaceful, enjoyable prelude to what's always a long and busy day. It's a little bit of therapy, if you will, to make that ten- to fifteen-minute drive, see the cars with Buckeye flags hoisted, witness the fall colors in the trees, see the parking lots in grocery stores buzz with excitement, and then as you get closer to the stadium see the activity increase. Whether you drive in along Olentangy River Road, come along Lane Avenue, or take one of the side roads off High Street, it's an opportunity to soak up a fair amount of Buckeye mania.

On this morning prior to the Michigan game, it was considerably different. The cold air certainly sparked the senses, even after a late evening. The normally quiet morning at home and the solitude of the ride in the car were anything but. After rousing my overnight visitors, loading up the trunk of the car with tailgating essentials, and making sure that everyone had more than enough cold weather gear, the ride to the stadium began with passengers squeezed into my car. The traffic into the assigned parking location on the west side of Ohio Stadium took, understandably, more time than normal.

When running on schedule, my pregame routine usually involves strolling around St. John Arena, where our flagship station, WBNS-AM, stages a local pregame tailgate show. Also, our network affiliate from Lima, WIMA, stages a similar setup, and usually I will stroll by and see the guys from Lima, Vince Koza, and Todd Walker, and just chat with them about their previous night's high school broadcasts and about the coming Buckeye game. These guys usually travel to most of the away games also, and it's a blast hearing their travel stories. The morning routine is a chance to just kind of see what the fans see and just take things easy for a little bit.

On this morning, taking that simple walk was a tad more challenging with the human crush of people who had descended upon the campus and tailgate areas. After making a brief on-air appearance at our station location, the friends whom I had walked with and who had been standing just to the side of the stage were completely lost from my sight just ten minutes later. The swarm of bodies erased them from where I had any chance to locate them. Fortunately, they were prepared to move on with the rest of their day.

During the last half of the season, the folks from Tostitos had been present at Ohio State home games, passing out free samples of their chips. Tostitos, of course, purchased the naming right for the Fiesta Bowl, and they were pushing their product on the OSU campus for their connection to the national championship game. On the day of the Michigan game, there were people walking around with Tostitos "Chip Hats." These things were big, gaudy, and very noticeable. However many they had brought weren't enough, because there were people asking anyone who would listen how they could get one of those hats. Eventually one of my houseguests managed to talk some young tailgater into selling his "Chip Hat." He never did admit how much cash he had to fork over for that hat, but it still serves as a great memory of his day at the Michigan game.

Kickoff!

After all the hoopla and all the anticipation, it was time for the matter to be decided on the field. A record-setting crowd settled into Ohio Stadium, as well as others watching on TV (and we hoped listening on the radio) as the Buckeyes went about trying to clinch a spot in the national championship game. This game started much like the previous few had for Ohio State.

Although the presence of freshman tailback Maurice Clarett seemed at first to energize the offense, they still struggled to make anything happen. Clarett did manage a two-yard touchdown run in the second quarter, but there was little to yell about when Ohio State had the ball. The Buckeye defense continued to hold up its end of the deal and keep Michigan from taking advantage of the offensive weakness. Three Wolverine first-half drives ended up as Adam Finley field goals. Ohio State found itself trailing 9-7 as the season and the dream moved into the final quarter. All who had suffered frayed nerves and tension in the last few weeks with these Buckeyes had to once again endure high drama.

You could tell that those in the stands were just waiting to erupt. Waiting for something good to happen to this team that had managed to find a way, week after week to survive. The decisive drive that settled this game involved a number of key plays. Fullback Brandon Schnittker hauled in a 15-yard pass to keep this crucial drive going in Michigan territory. It was a pass intended for Michael Jenkins, but Schnittker reached and collared it. This contribution was significant in that the fullback had been such a little-used weapon all season long. Schnittker and Brandon Joe had shared time at the position, and both had been given very little chance to the handle the ball. Their main responsibility, as it has been seemingly for ages at Ohio State, is to clear the way for the tailbacks. Both had performed well in the blocking capacity. It was indeed a surprise when at this crucial point of the game, Schnittker found himself in the center of the battle. Fortunately when we gathered in a ball meant for someone else, he made the play that was needed.

The game was approaching the five-minute mark of the fourth quarter. The crowd still hungered with anticipation. Dreams hinged on this drive.

Another key play. On fourth down, one yard to go, Buckeye quarterback Craig Krenzel continued to show his toughness and squirted behind his blockers to secure the much-needed first down to the Michigan 32. As Ohio State lined up to run this fourth and one, it brought back memories of a year before, when on fourth and one from just past the 50-yard line, Johnathan Wells needed just one yard for a first down. He slipped through everyone and scored a touchdown that set the tone in the Buckeyes' win in Ann Arbor in 2001. This first down by Krenzel didn't register six points, but it was HUGE!

Then, on the very next play, Krenzel sailed a pass to Clarett, and the hard-pounding runner used his athletic ability to gather in the ball and motor to the Michigan six-yard line.

The dream was still alive! All hell was about to break loose!

With 4:55 left in the game, Ohio State reached back in time. The Buckeyes brought out the option play to the right and tossed to tailback Maurice Hall. The sophomore who scored the game-winning touchdown the week before against Illinois scooted for three yards that must have seemed like they were a mile long to every Ohio State fan. Hall hit the end zone. The Buckeyes scored their second TD of the day, the first TD of the second half. The pent up emotions exploded from those more than 100,000 fans in the Horseshoe. Ohio State had taken a 14-9 lead over Michigan and had less than five minutes to preserve the dream. Just like Purdue, just like Illinois, while everyone waited for the offense to strike, they delivered with the style of football made famous in the days of Woody Hayes to get the biggest score of the year. So much for all that "basketball on grass."

But the issue was far from being decided!

Michigan's hopes were still alive. It seemed as though Wolverine quarterback John Navarre had started to find his groove. The jubilation that most everyone in Ohio Stadium had felt following Hall's score turned to the same concern that had existed most of the day. The defense was once again being leaned on. Once again they delivered. Defensive end Darrion Scott forced Navarre to fumble the ball, and the other end, Will Smith, was there to recover the ball. The Buckeyes had possession at their own 36-yard line with a little more than two minutes to go. The concern once again shifted to euphoria. In our radio booth we joked about how a "first down or five" would go a long way. It was the hope that the offense could hog the ball and run the clock down to zeros.

Didn't happen! Just like at Illinois last week!

As he had been called on so many times, Andy Groom was needed to put Michigan as far back as he could and force the Wolverines to have to go coast to coast in their effort to be a dream killer. Groom's punt traveled 49 yards and was returned by Michigan to their own 20-yard line. The Buckeye defense had a little less than a minute to keep its opponents from traveling 80 yards. You liked their chances if you were an Ohio State fan, but remember, Navarre had been getting hot.

Navarre hit on a couple of key completions. Then a pass interference call against Chris Gamble aided the Michigan cause and added to the gray hairs of Buckeye fans. Down to the game's final nine seconds ... enough time for possibly one play, maybe two.

The Buckeye defense hunkered down to gut it out one last time. They had already come up with one late turnover. It was obvious that Michigan was going to have to pass. Navarre retreated to toss and went for the end zone and six points. Pressure caused Navarre to throw incomplete in the end zone, and as the ball fell incomplete, there was more anticipation of the dream being realized. But not quite yet!

I can remember when the pass fell incomplete. In our booth, Jim Lachey let out a big yell on the air. For any who have listened to our broadcasts, you know that Jim gets very excited on the air when big things happen. For that matter, Jim Karsatos on the sideline is the same way. This yell from Jim Lachey, at first, had me thinking that a penalty flag had been dropped and that possibly Ohio State had been called for pass interference or any infraction that would have prevented the game from ending and allowed Michigan to have a free play. Maybe there was a flag dropped that I hadn't seen but Jim had. That wasn't why he yelled. There were still two seconds left on the game clock, and he was shocked that there was any time remaining. Michigan had one more chance.

The anxiety for Buckeye fans continued.

Michigan had the ball at the Ohio State 24-yard line. The season, the dreams, and everything that had occurred in the previous 12-plus weeks came down to this game and to this final play. It certainly wasn't new territory for Ohio State, following the previous week's game in Champaign. All you could do was keep taking deep breaths. I can recall thinking about all of these players on the field for both teams and wondering if each and every one of them took a second to think that this, indeed, was the type of setting that most every kid who ever plays sports dreams about. You can imagine that every fan in the stands or in other places dreamed at one time or another about the possibility of a season being decided on one play and your favorite team pulling it out. Certainly coaches prepare for these situations. The Ohio State coaching staff has a drill called "Last play in the world" that they use in practice. So, being unable to avoid using an overused cliché, the season came down to ONE FINAL PLAY!

Navarre dropped back to throw … and once the ball was in the air it seemed suspended in time, with all waiting for it fall toward the ground and the players waiting to catch it, steal it, or knock it down. The pass was intended for Braylon Edwards, who was cutting toward the goal line from the left side of the field. Then all of a sudden a scarlet flash came toward the ball, and safety Will Allen had intercepted it! He had gotten his hands on the ball near the goal line, and his momentum carried him to about the five-yard line. Quite honestly, in the booth, I couldn't even see who it was that had picked the pass off. Allen's number 26 on the front of his jersey was obscured by the way he was hugging the ball to make sure it didn't pop loose. It was impossible to see the number on the back of his jersey right away because his defensive teammates jumped on his back immediately! It wasn't until after a moment or so when Jim Lachey had seen a TV replay that we realized it was Allen. The game was finally over, and Ohio State beat Michigan 14-9 to end the season unbeaten at 13-0. Once the game was over, the first thought that occurred was the first thing I said on the air, "The Buckeyes are headed to the desert!"

After all the tension and anxiety, after all the key plays and timeouts extending the mystery, and after all the close calls in a season full of close calls, Ohio State had run the table and they were going to play for the national championship. It was a moment to savor, but it was also a moment, much like most of the season, that left you speechless and breathless.

It was still a hard thought to fathom, as we sat there in the cold in Columbus, Ohio watching this game come to an end that we would have the chance in less than two months to call the national championship game and see the continued chase for an accomplishment that hadn't been realized in over 30 years for this proud football program and its very loyal and proud fans. It was also very hard to catch your breath. This wonderful moment in sports that everyone was trying to put in perspective had been very close to being stopped. Add to that it was now being enjoyed at the expense of Ohio State's biggest rival, who had broken so many Buckeye hearts and dreams so many times before.

It was the second time in this season of narrow escapes that Will Allen had come to the rescue in the final moments. You'll remember he intercepted the last pass of the game thrown by Cincinnati, killing their bid for an upset of the Buckeyes. The junior from Huber Heights Wayne High School in the Dayton area had been used as the Buckeye's fifth defensive back all season long.

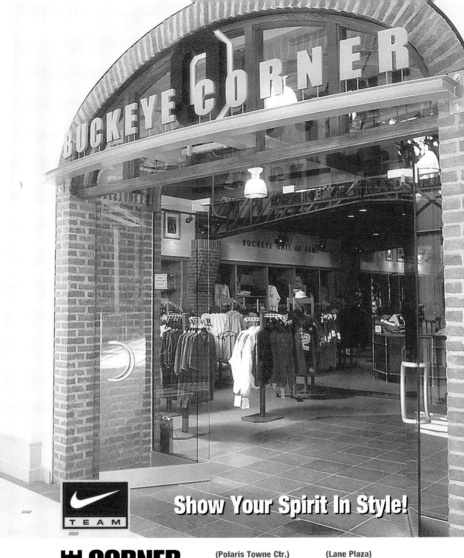

Show Your Spirit In Style!

"I knew number 80 [Edwards] was going to be there, because he's their go-to-guy," said Allen. "But they shouldn't have done it. They shouldn't have gone his way."

The Ohio State players had done a wonderful job all season long keeping a solid emotional balance, just like their head coach. They basked in their earlier success, but also kept it in perspective and put their attention right away on the next matter at hand. Knowing now that they would have weeks before another game, they let the emotions flow, and a season's worth of excitement was cut loose. "We knew it was going to be a close game," said quarterback Craig Krenzel. "We knew they were going to come in and play us tough and that it would be a physical battle. The way our season has gone, the fact it came down to the last play, that's no surprise."

"It's a dream come true to get to this point," said linebacker Matt Wilhelm, who had 15 tackles in the game. " We've obviously got one left, one big one left. We've attained some of the goals we talked about earlier in the season, but the big one is still left."

Celebration

Once Will Allen's interception ended the Ohio State-Michigan game, it touched off a celebration like none seen in Ohio Stadium in many a moon, certainly not since the Horseshoe was renovated. The Buckeye players were caught up in the moment as soon as Will Allen fell to the ground at the five-yard line, but they were quickly joined by thousands who had streamed from the stands to join in on the partying. There had been concern regarding fans charging the field, and there was a very noticeable presence of police and security personnel on the field … but what they aimed much of their focus at was the goal posts in the stadium.

I don't know if it's true, but we were told early that morning that the goal posts had been greased with motor oil and that police would do all they could to keep revelers from trying to uproot them. These goal posts, however, are set pretty deep into the ground, and the word was that it would be damn near impossible to get those things taken down, even if folks got on top of them. Unfortunately there were some fools who got by the police and mounted the goal posts. They spent quite of bit of time enjoying themselves while hanging onto the goal posts, but were unsuccessful in bringing them down.

A majority of the people who went onto the field after the game were there to enjoy the moment. They slapped the backs of players, traded high-fives with one another. Some took hunks of grass as keepsakes, but most were just celebrating a great win by the Buckeyes to cap off a season for the ages. It was just the start of the night's festivities.

But the sight of all those people on the field from up in the press box was like nothing I had ever seen. All of those people, all of that scarlet and gray, and all of the hysteria was a once-in-a-lifetime moment that I know I'll never forget. While those on the field got your visual attention, there were still tons of fans who remained in the safety of their seats, but were doing just as much celebrating over this great moment.

It usually takes us about an hour to and hour and a half before we wrap up our postgame broadcast duties. The sounds coming from the locker room and the interview areas were priceless. Most notably, the officials from the Fiesta Bowl were on hand to extend the official invitation to Ohio State to play in the January 3 game in Tempe, Arizona. Once the gentlemen in their bright yellow sportcoats offered the invite, Jim Tressel, whom Buckeye fans and followers had come to know as a very eloquent wordsmith, offered just two simple words, "We accept!" Probably the briefest statement made by the Buckeye coach since accepting the Ohio State coaching job.

Once our work in the booth was done, it was time for our radio crew to celebrate. Going all the way back to the season opener against Texas Tech in August, Jim Karsatos and I had begun loading up coolers with various beverages, and snacks and making sure there were lawn chairs so that once we got done in the press box, we could enjoy a little of the tailgating that most Buckeye fans take advantage of several hours ahead of us. It was just a way for our little group to blow off some steam after a long day, before heading home or to points elsewhere. From week one throughout the entire 2002 home schedule, we gathered in the parking lot just west of the stadium for our little postgame gathering. This event, however, became popular among friends of our working party and word soon started to spread that the radio announcers had a regular tailgate thing going.

Pretty soon, some employees of the university would stop by, spouses of those in our work group, former players, some of my relatives who live in the Columbus area, as well as friends from Cincinnati who would attend some of the games. There were even times that people none of us knew would join the gatherings. There was some guy named Dave, whom nobody knew at first, but he kept showing up, and we just did our best to make him feel at home. It sometimes made for an interesting mix. Following the Michigan game, it was a very festive but cold gathering. You could definitely tell there was something different in the air. While darkness fell and the weather got even colder, people couldn't help but keep talking about the unbelievable season that had just concluded, and craving the warm weather of Tempe, Arizona, and a shot at linking the past generation of 1968 to the present-day Buckeye thrills.

We stayed in that parking lot for hours, just mulling over every piece of this day. Players, coaches, fans and even security people walked past our gathering, and everyone had a greeting, or an "O-H-I-O" chant, or some sign that this was a special day and evening. It didn't matter all that much how dark it got or how cold it was; it was a day that wouldn't long be forgotten. It would be weeks before any such gathering by any Ohio State football fans and followers would occur, but this would be the last time during the magical 2002 season that we would be able to bond in the shadow of Ohio Stadium, where just a few months ago people were complaining about it being too damn hot.

There was no rush to end this special day!

CHAPTER 4
THE FIESTA BOWL

Spoiling It for Everyone

While it was a special day when Ohio State beat Michigan, clinching the invite to the Fiesta Bowl, there were those whose foolish act cast a bit of tarnish on the day. During that Saturday, people were cutting loose and having the time of their lives, and there's no way to say that everyone did so like angels. But as the evening rolled along, it seemed that for the most part, everyone was putting his or her best showing forward.

It was nice to eventually get back home after the game and enjoy the evening with a few close friends and houseguests. Of those who were on hand, everyone had been at the stadium all day and sitting out in the cold. No one was really anxious to get back out. Relaxing and taking it easy was the main objective. Once the 11 p.m. news came on television, there was curiosity about how the rest of the night was pro-

Ohio State fans sit on one of the goal posts at Ohio Stadium. The win over Michigan gave the Buckeyes a perfect 13-0 season, a share of the Big Ten title and a shot at the national championship.

gressing, especially around the campus area, where there was a great deal of concern about possible problems, mostly because of incidents that had occurred in the past. Even leading up to the game, school and city officials had urged Buckeye supporters to act properly. At the time of the evening newscasts on TV, other than isolated incidents, things seemed to be, for the most part, orderly.

Then the next morning, word of later events made you realize that unfortunately, there were some fools who brought the celebration a bad image. It's not like Columbus was the only place during the course of this football season to experience such problems, but it got a great deal of attention, some of it from a national standpoint. It's unfortunate that the acts of some had to cast a dark tone on what had been such a great accomplishment by the football team.

Waiting On an Opponent

While Ohio State was fortunate enough to know where and when they would play next, they were going to have to wait a few weeks to find out whom they'd face in the Fiesta Bowl. The defending national champion Miami Hurricanes were the only remaining unbeaten team left in Division 1-A, but they had two more games remaining. They would face Syracuse in the Carrier Dome and then close the regular year at home against Virginia Tech.

On paper, neither of these games figured to be much trouble for Larry Coker's team. All the while, Ohio State fans were anxious to see if someone could pull off the upset. On the one hand you wanted a shot at knocking off the champs;

however, on the other, the chances of winning in the Fiesta Bowl might be easier against someone else. There was also a third line of thought. Even if Miami lost one of their final two games, it was a strong possibility that they could still be placed in the Fiesta Bowl, but as the number-two team, with Ohio State rated number one. A Hurricane loss, however, would also create the possibility of someone else getting the nod to face the Buckeyes, choosing from the field of other one-loss teams like Iowa or Oklahoma. Those two options presented their own ready-made story lines.

A matchup with Iowa had not occurred in the regular season, with the Buckeye and Hawkeyes not appearing on one another's regular-season schedule for the previous two years. Although Iowa had one defeat against Iowa State, they had managed to remain perfect in league play, as had the Buckeyes, resulting in a Big Ten shared title between the two schools. There was even one national sportscaster who kept proclaiming that Iowa was the most talented team in the Big Ten, more so than Ohio State, helping fuel some of the talk about the two teams from the same conference and how nice it would be for them to settle the issue on a national stage. But Iowa needed Miami to lose one of those remaining games to have a shot at this possible dream matchup.

Oklahoma found itself needing similar help as well to possibly get a shot at the Buckeyes. The Sooners were saddled with one loss also, and a possible Oklahoma-Ohio State matchup created some ready-made headlines as well. Sooner head coach Bob Stoops, who had coached his team to a national title in his second year, was a native Ohioan from Youngstown. Of course, Jim Tressel enjoyed massive success while coaching at Youngstown State. That was just one of the stories that could have occurred had Oklahoma had a chance to square off against Ohio State.

All of that speculation became a moot point, however. Miami blasted the Orangemen in Syracuse 49-7 and then beat Virginia Tech in the finale 56-45 in a game in which tailback Willis McGahee rushed for six TDs. The Hurricanes jumped out to a huge lead against the Hokies in that game, but Virginia Tech kept clawing back, making it a little more interesting than you would have thought before the game was over. Certainly the thought ran through the minds of more than one Buckeye fan about whether or not Ohio State's coaches could gain any insight into how to attack Miami based on what happened late in the VT game.

So the card was set. Number-one Miami and number-two Ohio State would meet for the national championship in Tempe. The last time these two schools got together on the football field was the start of the 1999 year in the Kickoff Classic in East Rutherford, New Jersey. Miami won that game. There were a few players on each team who were there that day in New Jersey. Hurricane quarterback Ken Dorsey was a backup to Kenny Kelly. Mike Doss, Matt Wilhelm, Donnie Nickey and Kenny Peterson were part of that Ohio State team, which eventually finished the year without going to a bowl game. Both teams had changed head coaches since then.

The most recent and notable get-together between these two teams in a major sports venue was the 2000 NCAA South Region second-round game in Nashville, where the basketball Buckeyes were eliminated from the postseason by Miami.

Tickets, Anyone? Part II

Once the Ohio State Buckeyes had beaten Michigan and accepted the invitation to the Fiesta Bowl, the hunt was on for game tickets, as well as airfare to Phoenix, Arizona, for the January 3 game. There had been a fair number of Buckeye fans who seemed to get a head start on airfares, in the hopes that Ohio State might make it. There were a lot of people who had done the same thing in 1998 when Ohio State was unbeaten and ranked number one in the country for most of the year, until a November loss to Michigan State killed a chance at the Fiesta Bowl, which was also the title game that year. For those who had earlier bought plane tickets, it was being looked at as a holiday vacation if the Buckeyes didn't get to the title game.

Once the Michigan game ended, airfare to Phoenix reportedly increased right away.

"Airfare started to increase almost immediately from the time the Bucks beat Michigan until the Fiesta Bowl," said Columbus travel agent Pat Datillo. "I began checking that that night and airfare started at $348.00 per person. By mid-December, it was already at $728.00 and rising. By December 30, it was well over $1300.00 per person." In addition, Pat stated that even for fans who were willing to plunk down whatever cash it took, it still wasn't easy to fly to Arizona for the game. "There were no extra flights added to accommodate the fans, and the fact that airlines blacked out certain dates made it increasingly difficult to book travelers. People were at the mercy of the airlines, and supply and demand saw fares costing four times what they normally did." As a result there were many Ohio State fans who looked into other options, such as flying to other cities, like Las Vegas, then driving into Phoenix.

Tickets for the game became the toughest item to chase down. The seats, which were going for around $150, were few in number. It's not all that unusual for me or some of my colleagues to get requests for tickets. Sometimes people even offer to pay for them (as opposed to those who think you can get them freebies)! It was always entertaining to get a phone call from someone you hadn't heard from in a year or so asking if you knew how they could get Fiesta Bowl tickets. There is an acquaintance of mine whom I only hear from every other year. It's the years in which Ohio State has Michigan at home, and the call is to ask if I know of any way that this person can purchase tickets to the Michigan game. It must have been my good fortune, because I heard from this person twice in the same calendar year—the annual call about Michigan tickets and also to ask about the possibility of Fiesta Bowl tickets. As "happy" as I was to hear from this person, you can imagine that I didn't extend myself too far trying to accommodate the request.

Even my mother, an Ohio State alum, asked me about getting her tickets!

The ticket chase even got so crazy that there were some Buckeye fans in Columbus who somehow made contact with the mayor of Tempe, asking if he could be of any help. In an interview on our radio station, Mayor Neil Giuliano relayed the story and how he attempted to be of assistance. "In my nearly nine years as mayor of Tempe, there has never been a hotter ticket than the 2003 national championship Fiesta Bowl.

I wish I had been in the position to provide tickets for all the Buckeye and Hurricane fans who called my office thinking I had some available.

"I could not even get tickets for some longtime friends of mine who are Buckeye fans who traveled to Tempe only to pay $500 a ticket just before game time," said Giuliano. "In retrospect, they were glad they bought when they did and got inside to see the collegiate national championship of a lifetime right here in Tempe."

Then there were those who just went, whether they had game tickets or not. They just wanted to be out there and soak up the experience. As you'll read later on, there was a lot to soak up.

Unfortunately, there were some who were so anxious to get tickets to the Fiesta Bowl that they fell prey to unsavory types looking to make a fast buck at the expense of somewhat desperate fans.

For those who did end up being victimized, some justice came to pass. A Utah man who had reportedly pried money from fans with bogus ticket sales by way of the internet was nabbed in June of 2003 in a Salt Lake City suburb after police stopped him for speeding. This man had offered tickets via the internet, and buyers needed to pay half the price in advance and then pick them up at either a hotel or restaurant in the Phoenix area.

According to various reports from media agencies, the individual told friends he had collected $80,000 for the tickets. Investigators claimed they found 93 different victims involving about $202,300. When the people who thought they had tickets showed up for the Fiesta Bowl, neither this ticket broker, nor the tickets, could be found.

Authorities had been searching for this individual ever since January and charged him with three second-degree felony counts of communications fraud. It was an unfortunate instance of someone trying to take advantage of the eagerness of those who wanted to be part of Ohio State's successful season.

Countdown to Tempe

All during the month of December, you couldn't help but have conversations with people either by phone or in person about whether they were going to the Fiesta Bowl and when they were leaving. Despite the excitement generated by Ohio State's pending date with Miami in Arizona, I had to turn my attention to the basketball season. It was going to be a good month of hoops before most of my co-workers and me would get a sniff of warm desert air. I mention this because Jim O'Brien's team was engaged in a very tough stretch of non-conference games, playing Alabama in the Hall of Fame Classic in Springfield, Massachusetts, then tangling with Duke in Greensboro, North Carolina and also a road game against Pittsburgh. It was also made difficult because of the injuries mentioned earlier to Shun Jenkins and Brandon Fuss-Cheatham.

But all during the December stretch of basketball games, it seemed like the questions about the football season and the Fiesta Bowl were more prominent. For example, on the day that we were getting ready to leave with the basketball team for their game in Pittsburgh, another of my co-workers asked, "When are you leaving?" I assumed she was asking about the hoops game and replied, "Later tonight." It was when she gave me a real strange look that I realized she wasn't asking about the basketball game, but about the Fiesta Bowl.

The Christmas season brought even more discussion of the Fiesta Bowl trip. So many people seemed to have plans to go. It was very flattering that so many folks wanted to make contact and say, "Let's get together in Arizona for dinner, or a beer, or something." There were even calls from a few acquaintances in the Phoenix area who wanted to try to get together. What was difficult was having to explain to all of these people that it wasn't likely to happen. Jim Lachey and Jim Karsatos and I weren't leaving for the January 3 game until January 1. Then the whole day on the second was going to be taken up with on-air responsibilities. Then we were leaving early in the morning right after the game to return home. There was even an invitation to join some of the people on our sales staff for a gathering, but we had to pass on that also. It was a nice problem to have, but after all, for us it was work.

Once the Ohio State football team left for Arizona right around Christmas, reality hit. They took the approach of a business trip. After all, it was serious business. They were attempting to dethrone the national champions. They had maintained incredible focus during the 13-game regular season. Now after a little bit of a break, they were faced with regaining that focus to play the toughest opponent they would face all season. And without question, they would be viewed as underdogs.

Clarett Controversy

With the exception of some of the media who went to Arizona when the football team departed, most people back in Columbus and in Central Ohio were following what was going on with the Buckeyes from a distance. During the pre-Fiesta Bowl practices, Maurice Clarett grabbed the headlines in a way that many wished he hadn't.

While the team was in Arizona, Clarett attempted to get a plane ticket to return to Ohio and attend funeral services for a friend from Youngstown who had been shot to death. University officials said Clarett did not fill out the proper paperwork to qualify for NCAA emergency funds. Clarett responded angrily by claiming school officials gave him the "runaround," saying he had filled out the proper forms before the team left Ohio for Arizona. "They can't lie about that," said Clarett. "I won't sit here and let them lie about that."

In a university statement released in Arizona, director of athletics Andy Geiger said Clarett had not submitted a Free Application for Federal Student Aid Form to Ohio State (as of Monday, December 30). "Maurice may have begun the process," said Geiger, "but at the time we had to make the decision, there was no indication of a FAFFSA on file for Maurice. We were therefore compelled to follow the NCAA rules as they apply to the situation."

There was a prevailing piece of speculation regarding this incident among the media folks covering the Buckeyes during this time. First, that Clarett could have purchased the ticket himself, then applied for reimbursement for the funds after the fact. That's even giving benefit of the doubt that the

Fans line the streets in downtown Columbus to salute the Ohio State football team as they depart for the airport Thursday, December 26, 2002, before the Fiesta Bowl.

team would have given him permission to leave. Secondly, that buying the ticket himself was not what Clarett was prepared to do and wanted to do, and that he wanted the details taken care of by someone else. Again this was just speculation.

Another sticky wicket to this whole saga was that Clarett's friend died on December 21. He did not seek permission to return home until December 30, after the team was already in Arizona.

This brought attention to the Ohio State football team that no one wanted prior to this gigantic game. It wasn't the first time this had happened, with Clarett in the center of the storm. But the matter was eventually brushed aside, and life moved on in Tempe.

The Joys of Traveling

New Year's morning 2003! Day of departure for a group of four of us headed to Phoenix for our trip to the Fiesta Bowl. Fortunately, New Year's Eve involved a very quiet night at home. This also was when airports had stepped up security measures with X-raying checked luggage, so there was concern that the checking-in process would be even longer than it had been. That necessitated arriving at Port Columbus airport at least two hours before departure time. Being a nut for being early, I was there about two and a half hours ahead of time. But it was time well used, doing more prep work for the football game and diving into whatever the book of the week was.

I didn't really know how busy airports would be on New Year's Day, and the answer came quick: they were pretty busy. I was traveling with my two on-air partners for the football games, Jim Lachey and Jim Karsatos's along with Karsatos wife, Susan. We were all anxious to get the anticipated long day in airports over with, get to our hotel in Scottsdale, and get on with the process. We had no idea how long this day would become.

Our commercial flight arrangements had us flying into Detroit, then catching a connecting flight to Phoenix. (I won't mention airlines, and you'll soon see why.) We had about a 45-minute layover in Detroit before the next flight was to leave. Unfortunately, when we landed at Detroit Metro airport, the plane could not pull into its assigned gate. There was another aircraft at that gate in need of maintenance. We sat on the runway for over an hour, while our connecting flight left without us.

Then came the scramble of trying to get rebooked on another flight. Jim Lachey and I were able to get on another Detroit to Phoenix flight, but it didn't leave for about another five to six hours. Jim and Susan Karsatos were being booked on another route, which would give them another layover, in Minneapolis, before they would get to Arizona. To compound the problem, Jim and Susan ran into a ticket counter agent with a terrible attitude, just adding to the frustration of the whole mess.

By the time all four of us managed to get into Arizona, get our baggage and rental vehicle and motor to our hotel in Scottsdale, it was January 2. All the while, I kept thinking about all of those people who were green with envy about our

Ohio State tailback Maurice Clarett answers reporters' questions during a news conference before the Fiesta Bowl. Clarett was upset with school officials for failing to help him fly home to attend the funeral of a lifelong friend.

having the chance to go the Fiesta Bowl. In the long run, it certainly would work out, but man, was it frustrating. Things had to get better.

Arizona at Last

It was the day before the Fiesta Bowl, and the Valley of the Sun had been invaded by Buckeyes. When we arrived, you couldn't tell because of the darkness and the late hour, but the next day at the Scottsdale hotel that we were staying at—which also was where the football team was staying—it was Buckeye central. Throngs of fans, family members, and university personnel, as well as players and coaches, were all about the hotel grounds. You couldn't swing a dead cat and not hit someone wearing an Ohio State T-shirt or a Buckeye necklace.

The other very noticeable discovery was the business-like attitude of the football personnel, be they players or coaches. You saw groups of players moving about the hotel on their way to meetings or meals and doing so in a very orderly fashion. Same for coaches and others connected with the day-to-day function of the team. It was just as though you'd come across them in the Woody Hayes football complex in Columbus, business as usual.

At one point during this day, I happened across linebackers coach Mark Snyder and defensive backs coach Mel Tucker in one of the outside courtyard areas. They both had earlier appeared on our radio show from the hotel. While they took the time to chat and be their usual personable selves, it was obvious that they were ready for business.

While those key characters in this story were taking care of their duties, there were numerous others filling up the hotel swimming pools, restaurants, and gift shops having an absolute ball. While these Buckeye fans were there for a football game, they were also hungry for as much fun and excitement that a trip to the national championship game and tropical weather could provide, and many were gorging themselves on it.

From a working standpoint, we had quite a bit to do. There was the matter of catching up with Coach Tressel and recording the usual pregame interview. During the regular season, there's a routine that I have with Jim to get the interviews needed. It's a routine that we establish once the season is about to start. Having just arrived the night before (or was it the same morning, I'm not sure), there was still some question as to how some of this would get done. Coach Tressel was to spend one hour of a three-hour show on the air with us, and it was the hope that prior to whatever hour that would be, we could knock the pregame show out. Our executive producer, Skip Mosic, had been in Arizona all week, working on the afternoon talk show that was being done from the team hotel and chasing down interviews from press conferences. Skip had done what he could to try to plant the seed with getting everything setup. There would just naturally be a certain number of unknowns in this situation. That's why earlier I mentioned the inability to make social plans with other visitors from Ohio.

The day before the game, the excitement was building. People walked around with a noticeable bounce in their step, chanting "O-H-I-O" all throughout the hotel. Mostly you could tell people were enjoying being in the warm weather. And you could see people expressing their sincere best wishes to the players.

As the day moved on and the shows we were doing wound down, we were looking at about 24 hours to kickoff, and most of the work responsibilities were finished. I had one last task that needed to be performed on that day: getting a one-on-one interview with one of the players. The university staff, as you could imagine, was being very particular about players doing interviews in the hotel this close to game time. There had been a plan, however, to get this last interview done. Once again, Skip Mosic had gone through the proper channels in asking about this and making mention that I would need to grab someone. It had been indicated that once the players came back from their final walk-through, something could get done.

Then another curveball got thrown into the mix. The team returned from their walk-through earlier than what had been indicated. Players were heading off to their rooms or to spend time with their families who had come to Arizona. Once I got the phone call in my room that they were back early, I knew that getting someone for an interview would be a problem. There again was the concern about just stopping a player cold, who might not know that we had been given permission to do so. This left me walking around the lobby, passing through the conference center, where team meetings were occurring, hoping to get lucky and find somebody. While doing all of this nervous pacing, one of the staff members came to my rescue.

In the conference center I came across Mark Quisenberry, the video coordinator for the football team. He was in his first season working at Ohio State, and I had gotten to know Mark from our weekly Thursday afternoon call-in show with Coach Tressel at the Woody Hayes complex. Mark was always kind enough to let Jim Lachey and me see the video highlight package that would be shown to the team each game day morning at their team breakfast. It happened early in the season, and Mark kind of joked about it being a superstitious thing and that we had to keep seeing the video each week. It was a really neat experience to see the great work that Mark had done with highlights of the previous week's game and how he tied music to it.

While roaming the conference center that night before the game, I ran into Mark, and he asked who was I looking for. After explaining that I needed to get a player for a pregame interview and couldn't find anyone, Mark provided a solution. Two players were sitting in one of the conference rooms watching film of Miami. They were linebacker Matt Wilhelm and defensive tackle Tim Anderson, on their own, just the two of them. Matt was someone I had interviewed a few times during the year for the same segment, including the week of the Michigan game, so when Mark offered to ask if they would be willing to do the interview, I asked if he would try Tim. A moment later, Mark came from the room and said that Tim would be willing, just go right on in!

Now think about this for a minute. Here I am trying to get an interview and going into a room with two of Ohio State's starting defensive players who are taking extra time watching film of their opponent, getting ready for the biggest game of their lives, which would kick off in 24 hours. To say the least, I felt like I was intruding on an inner sanctum in which I did not belong!

Fortunately, and very graciously, Tim Anderson let me interview him while he and Matt Wilhelm sat there watching the tape. Not only was I very obliged to him granting the interview, I was even more impressed with these two young men and their dedication. These were guys who've made big plays, who were well established by what they had done on the field. You had to imagine that by this point in time, they had probably watched tons of tape on Miami, either in a full team setting or among their position groups. But here they were, looking for more of an edge, trying however they could to find a way to best their opponent. It was a chance to see a little bit of something that you wouldn't normally get to see. It's no wonder these two young men have been able to enjoy success on the field.

Finally, the workday was done. It was very much a relief. There now was time to enjoy a little of what most everyone else was experiencing in their Fiesta Bowl trip. Greg Snapp and his wife, Michelle, had extended an invitation to a gathering at a nearby home of some transplanted Ohioans. Greg works with our radio group on game day, holding the parabolic microphone (jokingly referred to as the "Salad Bowl") on the sideline during the game. Along with Skip Mosic and two very dear friends of mine, Mary and Doug Miles, who had come from Columbus for the game, we got a chance to attended this gathering to just blow off a little steam after a long day and before another one that was coming.

The reason that I mention this gathering is because someone involved in hosting this event was involved with the Fiesta Bowl committee—I'm not quite sure what the connection was. But they had arranged for the national championship trophy to be brought to this party and displayed for a brief period of time to visitors. Sadly, we didn't get there in enough time to see the trophy; we had to rely on everyone else's descriptions of how exquisite it was! Also we were told that the trophy had bodyguards accompanying it. We did get a chance to see Polaroids of the trophy, showing how beautiful it was, how large it was, and how the diamonds gave it more appeal. Fortunately, that wouldn't be the last time that trophy would be displayed to a group from Ohio.

Game Day

It was finally here, Friday, January 3, 2003. The day that Ohio State would play Miami for the national championship. The buzz around the team hotel got even stronger on that day. While the swimming pools and restaurants and lobbies in the hotel still resembled a vacation setting, it was obvious that the event that brought everyone to town was getting closer.

Other than taking a couple of hours to review the prep work that I had already done, this day allowed for a little bit of freedom. There was a chance to meet up with some relatives who live in the Phoenix area for a little while. Time to walk the grounds of the hotel and soak up some of the warm weather. Generally, when people ask if the Fiesta Bowl trip was fun, I have said in the past that other than the game, no it wasn't. But it wasn't intended to be fun; it was work. You know going in that free time is very limited. But I think back on that day of the football game and the time before leaving to go to the stadium, and it was a strange mixture of enthusiasm about the football game, the thrill of working at such a big event, the concern of making sure that I had done everything I could to be ready, the calm before the event, and the not-so-thrilling thought of having to pack and be ready for another early-morning departure and all-day adventure of traveling back home the next morning.

For some of my other comrades, the work day was starting much earlier than for me. Skip Mosic, D.R. Railsback, Jason Knapp, Ian Fitzsimmons and Jeff Austin all left for the stadium hours before I did. They had to get through security, set up equipment, and check everything out so that when the last three of us got there, we were ready to roll. D.R. and Jason had just come into town the day before the game, so they were really operating on short turnaround.

By mid-afternoon, it was time for Jim Lachey, Jim Karsatos, and me to drive to Sun Devil Stadium. The drive usually takes 20 to 25 minutes, but we anticipated heavy traffic and tried to figure that in. The freeway was clogged with people heading to the game. At one point we made the decision to leave the freeway and take a main road into Tempe. It was still a crawl, and what was even more amazing was that as we got close to the stadium, we saw very little police presence for traffic control. Maybe we're just spoiled by how the police in Columbus handle more than 100,000 people on home Saturdays.

The other thing we noticed, which shouldn't have been surprising, but was a sight to behold, was the swarm of Buckeye fans. It was as if you were going to a game in Ohio Stadium! Cars with OSU flags, people walking down the sidewalks with their Ohio State garb on. Made you wonder if anyone was left back in Ohio. Every now and again we saw a Hurricane fan, but they were far outnumbered.

Once we got to the stadium, parked and headed inside, it was obvious right away this was a big event. The crowds gathered around the stadium told you that, as well as the intense security to get into Sun Devil Stadium. Ever since the tragic events of 9/11, we all know that going through stepped-up security is a way of life. It became even clearer in attending a national championship game. But after all that, the traffics delays, and everything else, we were there. The reality of it all was getting stronger.

Sun Devil Stadium

More than 70,000 people would be on hand to watch this game. Sun Devil Stadium has been the home locale for Arizona State University, for the Fiesta Bowl dating back to when it was played between Christmas and New Year's, serves as the home field for the Arizona Cardinals, and has been ever since that team moved from St. Louis. It's a facility that has hosted a Super Bowl and has generally been regarded as a very good place to stage a big football game.

This would be the third time that Ohio State would play in the Fiesta Bowl. Twice during the 1980s the Buckeyes were invited to the game, losing to Penn State and defeating Pittsburgh. Both of my on-air partners had been part of the Buckeye team that beat Pitt. For Jim Lachey, he had been there numerous times as a member of the NFL's Washington Redskins, who were in the same division as the Cardinals. The last time Jim was in this stadium was not a good experience. "I was cleated by a teammate in the leg. I didn't think much of it until I looked down at my sock and saw blood," said Lachey, who ended up being taken to the hospital that day.

It was my second visit to Sun Devil Stadium. In the summer of 1996, while working as an announcer for the Cincinnati Bengals, I had been there for a preseason game. The one thing I remembered was that the press box was very, very high, at that time probably the highest I remembered ever being in. I remembered that it was tough at times to see players' numbers clearly. It was tough this night, but we had been somewhat trained for this. With the renovation at Ohio Stadium, the press box in Columbus was now much higher and farther away from the field than it had been. As a matter of fact, both the press boxes at Sun Devil Stadium and Ohio State are the highest and farthest away from the field of any that I can recall having visited.

Upon walking into the stadium on the night of the Fiesta Bowl, one of the first things that jumped out at me was how gaudy the Tostitos decorations all around the stadium were. The name, the colors that bordered the name, and the bag designs on some of the stadium facing jumped out at you and smacked you in the face. This isn't meant as any disrespect to the naming company, but there was no way you weren't going to know who the sponsor of this game was!

You also knew it was a big-time event once you did get to the press level. While we had seen a noticeable increase in media attendance at the Ohio State-Michigan game in Columbus one month prior, the mass of humanity in the press level on this night was overwhelming. Not only media people, but what must have been a combination of NCAA representatives, people from both the Big Ten and Big East conferences, and even people I knew from other universities (other than Ohio State and Miami) were there. The crunch of people in the press area reminding me of similar turnouts at Final Fours, Super Bowls and World Series games that I had attended.

Another sight that I won't forget is when they opened the stadium gates and let the fans in. It became apparent pretty quickly that this gathering of more than 70,000 people would be dominated by those wearing Scarlet and Gray and cheering for the Buckeyes. People had been hanging around the stadium area all day, just waiting for the gates to open. It seemed at times that you were watching fans filter into Ohio Stadium in the fall rather than Sun Devil Stadium in January.

Pregame

As the activity around Sun Devil Stadium heightened, it was time to start thinking about the game itself. While everyone had been offering their opinions for about a month on what it would take for Ohio State to win, or if they even had a chance, opinions were in abundance around the press box and on the field as to what might occur in this tilt.

As part of our pregame show, I had the chance to interview Joe Zagacki, who is the radio play-by-play voice of the Miami Hurricanes. It's a regular routine to interview one of the announcers from the opposing team. Our paths last crossed when these two teams played in August of 1999 in the Kickoff Classic. A lot had changed for both football programs in that time.

"There's no way this team is as good as last year," were some of Joe's first comments regarding the comparisons the current-day Hurricanes and the squad that took all the marbles against Nebraska in the Rose Bowl one year earlier. "There's a lot of respect for Ohio State. What would have Miami concerned is Ohio State's ability to tackle, Ohio State's ability not to give up the big play, and the way they are stingy inside the red zone. On the other side of the ball would be their perseverance with the running game."

There was also no shortage of celebrity types on the sideline all evening, leading up to the kickoff. One of them was Sean Salsbury, former quarterback at USC and in the NFL, now an analyst with ESPN. We were fortunate enough to get Sean's take on the upcoming game in an interview on the field with fellow Californian Jim Karsatos.

"If Ohio State's in it early, I think we'll be able to tell a quarter, quarter and a half into it," said Salsbury regarding the Buckeyes' chances. "And if Ohio State hits them in the mouth for a few turnovers, I think it's gonna be a close game. I think if it's close at halftime, Ohio State wins."

You may recall the earlier mention of a pregame interview with Ohio State defensive lineman Tim Anderson about this game. One of his keys was how strong was the faith the

Buckeye defensive players had in one another. "To be successful, every guy on the field has to do his job and not worry about the guy next to him. That's what our defense does; we've gained confidence in one another."

"Obviously, McGahee is a dangerous person," were Anderson's thoughts on the Hurricane offense they would face. "We've got to be able to go in there and shut down the run, but at the same time, we're gonna have to be able to defend the pass, because they can throw the ball pretty well, too."

What would pregame prognostications be without the thoughts of the two head coaches? Larry Coker had been an assistant at Ohio State under John Cooper and had a great deal of respect from his firsthand experience with the program, and even more with the team he was preparing for on this night.

"They obviously have a great defensive football team. I think we'll have to do a great job with our offensive line, and our defensive line will have to win those battles to stop their fine running game." While commenting on the Buckeye offense, Coker made certain to single out quarterback Craig Krenzel. "I think he's the trump card in the whole scenario, because he's such an effective player."

Also remember that going into this game, Larry Coker had never lost as Miami's head coach in 24 outings.

Coaching in a championship game was nothing new for Ohio State head coach Jim Tressel. He had reached the highest of levels during his time coaching the Penguins of Youngstown State at the 1-AA level. "What we've got to do is make sure that tonight, our emotional gas tanks are topped full."

As he looked toward the game and facing Miami's attack, Tressel stated, "The ability to adjust and make sure we do it for sixty minutes will be key. Everyone that has a chance to make a big play needs to make a big play this evening. That's what a championship game is all about."

But Tressel also knew that his team would be facing a challenge unlike any they had seen during the season. "Our defense is facing the most explosive, balanced offensive football team they have faced all year. They're excited about the task, they love great matchups. It's gonna be fun to watch our defense work."

And of course, the Buckeye head coach always puts a premium on special teams. "I don't think you can win a championship without winning in the special teams."

Kickoff!

After all the hoopla, the buildup, the interviews, the speculation and everything else, it was time for the national championship to be decided on the field.

Miami won the coin toss, but deferred. The OSU offense that so many had found fault with and had at times seemed to save their best moments for the final seconds would begin the night with the ball. Right before kickoff, Jim Lachey commented,

"I'm tired of talking about what could happen. Let's talk about what's gonna happen."

After the opening kickoff resulted in a touchback, Ohio State got the night off to suspicious start when they were penalized for having too many players on the field for their first play from scrimmage. That set the tone for this possession. The Buckeyes went three downs and punted. So the high-powered Miami offense took over. Among the many concerns for Ohio State was to keep the Miami offense from exploding early. That had been a big key in the Hurricanes getting a number of their opponents out of sync early.

On Miami's first play from scrimmage, All-America quarterback Ken Dorsey got a taste of what he'd see all night. Ohio State defensive end Will Smith charged and dropped Dorsey at the Miami 15-yard line. Dorsey had been protected like royalty all season by his offensive line. The hope among the Buckeyes was that if they could get to him and show him pressure unlike anything he'd seen all season, that might slow their attack down. Former Ohio State and NFL quarterback Mike Tomzcak was on the sideline at this game, and after seeing the Buckeyes get early pressure on Dorsey, he was hoping for more of the same. "The defense is trying to set the tone here; they gotta hit that Dorsey in the mouth and break his jaw, " said Tomzcak.

Also during the first Hurricane possession, after they had secured two first downs, senior defensive lineman Kenny Peterson got into the act by sacking Dorsey behind the line—an indication as to how psyched up the Buckeye defensive line was for this night. Eventually, the Hurricanes had to surrender the ball by punting. Miami did manage to down that punt at Ohio State's one-yard line.

Possession changed again as Ohio State was unable to get a conversion. All-American Andy Groom punted from his own end zone, and Miami took over at their own 48-yard line. A key pass completion from Ken Dorsey to tight end

Kellen Winslow, Jr. got the Hurricanes to the OSU 25, but all the while Dorsey was taking hits and feeling pressure from the pass rush. Also, the defensive front early on was keeping Miami's Heisman finalist tailback Willis McGahee in check. In Miami's previous game, McGahee had run for six touchdowns against Virginia Tech. But Dorsey managed to strike through the air and tossed a 25-yard TD pass to Roscoe Parrish. He caught the ball at the five, coming off the right flank, and cut past Mike Doss for the first score of the night. Despite being knocked around early, the defending national champions had struck first, gaining a 7-0 edge.

Then it looked like Ohio State might be in more trouble. Following a touchback on the kickoff, Craig Krenzel was intercepted by Miami defensive back Sean Taylor. Krenzel was tossing for Chris Vance, but gave the ball to Miami at their own 35. Krenzel had only thrown five picks all season prior to that.

Miami kept trying to get McGahee on track, but all he saw was negative yardage. Their movement was through the air, but not enough, having to once again punt away and failing to take advantage of the turnover.

The second quarter started with Miami still up 7-0. With Ohio State gumming up Miami's hopes of establishing a run, Dorsey again went to the air on third and four from his own 29-yard line. As he tried for a long-range completion, cornerback Dustin Fox intercepted the pass. The Buckeyes had regained some momentum and had the ball inside the 50-yard line. It was again becoming obvious that the pass rush was bothering the Miami quarterback.

While McGahee was finding it tough to find running room, the same was happening to Ohio State's Maurice Clarett. But that didn't stop the Buckeyes from running. Quarterback Craig Krenzel started gashing the Hurricanes by running the ball.

A third-down rush by Krenzel got Ohio State inside Miami's 20, and on fourth and two, Mike Nugent lined up for a 35-yard field goal try. Before sending the field goal unit on, there was a lengthy discussion between Jim Tressel and his coaches on the sideline. At first, the guess was that they were discussing whether to try for the conversion rather than kick for the three points. Instead, they were calling for a fake field goal.

Punter Andy Groom, also the holder on kick placements, picked up the snap and ran to his right, trying to get the first down. It appeared Groom might also have had the option pitch to the kicker, Nugent.

"I don't think Mike would have gotten it, either," said Jim Karsatos from the sideline. "If there's any question about whether the Buckeyes are gonna be conservative, I guess that answers it," said Jim Lachey.

So Miami got the ball back, still up a touchdown. Still with not much of a rushing threat, Dorsey was trying to advance their possession by throwing. It got him in trouble again. On 3 and six from their own 34, Dorsey had a passed picked off by Buckeye All-America safety Michael Doss, who returned it inside the Hurricane 20-yard line. This was the second interception of the season for Doss, and after having yielded some momentum after the fake field goal play didn't work, it looked like the Buckeyes were back in business again. Linebacker Matt Wilhelm got into the field of vision of the Miami receiver, causing him problems, and linebacker Cie Grant was adding to the pressure that had been building on the Miami quarterback. Turnover number two.

A Krenzel-to-Chris Vance hookup gave Ohio State a first-and-goal situation at Miami's four-yard line. Then after some back and fourth, the Buckeyes were facing fourth and goal at the one-yard line. Krenzel, who had been stopped short on third down, punched it in from one yard out. His second rushing TD of the year, coupled with Nugent's point after, tied the game at 7-7, with about two and a half minutes to play before halftime.

Then on the very next play from scrimmage, after OSU had kicked off, Kenny Peterson continued the defensive harassment of Miami quarterback Ken Dorsey. On first and ten, with the Hurricanes at their own 20, Peterson slammed into Dorsey, popping the ball loose. Darrion Scott jumped on the pigskin, and just like that, Ohio State had come up with their third turnover. They also were threatening to score again, with possession of the ball at Miami's 14-yard line. It was the third straight possession that Miami had coughed up the football.

Then Maurice Clarett got into the act. His yards had been tough in coming, but he bruised his way into the end zone from seven yards out, for his 15th rushing TD of the year. Two scores in a matter of moments. The defense took the ball away from Miami the last three times they had it, and as the Buckeyes took a 14-7 lead into the locker room at halftime, it appeared the underdogs were carrying the fight. As he walked off the field at the half, head coach Jim Tressel commented, "Our defense has set up some great opportunities for us. We got in, got some points on the board, but this is gonna be a whale of a game for the next 30 minutes."

Coach Tressel was wrong. It would be more than 30 minutes.

Second Half

Miami started the second half with possession of the football, and Ohio State owned a 14-7 lead. The Buckeye defense had kept the Hurricanes under wraps; in particular, they had coaxed Ken Dorsey into spitting up the ball three times. They also had kept running back Willis McGahee from hurting them, but you had to figure this team was too good not to adjust at halftime and start finding ways to move the ball. But the half started much the way the first one had gone for Miami: having to punt the ball.

During OSU's first possession of the half, Jim Karsatos relayed a story from down on the field that quarterback Craig Krenzel and wide receiver Michael Jenkins had gotten into a shouting match in the first half. "Craig was telling Jenkins, 'You need to finish your route, that's why I keep on getting stuck having to run. Finish your route, I'll throw the ball, I have the faith'," said Karsatos from the field. "I think they're good in the second half."

The drive began at the OSU 28-yard line. They advanced to their own 48, the moved backward to the OSU 37. Then on third down, Krenzel went down the left sideline to Chris Gamble for 57 yards, giving the Buckeyes first and goal at the Miami six-yard line. The Buckeyes then went for Miami's jugular vein. Krenzel tossed into the end zone, looking for tight end Ben Hartsock, but the ball was intercepted by Miami defensive back Sean Taylor. It would be Taylor's second pick of the night, but it would set up one of the strangest plays of the game.

After coming out of the end zone with the ball, Taylor moved up the left sideline. As we watched from way up in the press box, it looked like the play ended when Taylor was knocked down at his own 26-yard line. But Ohio State's Maurice Clarett ripped the ball out of Taylor's hands, regaining possession for the Buckeyes just seconds after they had coughed the ball up.

"We got the ball back!" yelled Jim Lachey in the booth. "Great hustle by number 13 to come from behind and take the ball away." You could also easily see how upset Sean Taylor was with himself. He had made an outstanding play to intercept the ball, only to be guilty of Miami's fourth turnover of the night. Ohio State was back in business.

The Buckeyes had to then settle for a 44-yard field goal by Mike Nugent. This young man had come far from the inconsistency of his freshman season. He had set seven school kicking records along the way. Nugent calmly banged in a 44-yard field goal, giving Ohio State a 10-point lead over Miami, 17-7. With eight and a half minutes to play in the third quarter, the Buckeyes had avoided a disaster. This possession also allowed their defense to get some much-needed rest on the bench.

The enthusiasm over a 10-point lead fueled even more optimism among those with Buckeye ties. Former Ohio State quarterback and present-day ESPN college football analyst

Kirk Herbstriet was on the sideline for the game, saying, "The defense has dominated the game, taking McGahee out, which we all talked about being a key, which allows you to put pressure on Dorsey."

Again, you just knew Miami would be heard from. And they were. Dorsey kept going to tight end Kellen Winslow, Jr. The Buckeyes were having a hard time keeping Winslow in check. It reminded you of the 2000 season, when Ohio State lost in a shootout with Purdue in West Lafayette. That was the game in which the Boilermakers went ahead for good on a long Drew Brees-to-Seth Morrales TD pass. It was the Buckeyes' inability to stop Purdue tight end Tim Stratton that proved costly. The way Miami was utilizing Winslow was much the same.

Miami used the combination of Dorsey's ability to hit Winlsow and runs by Willis McGahee to march down the field. Then with a little more than two minutes to play in the third quarter, McGahee scored on a nine-yard run, his 28th rushing TD of the year. That, plus the point after, cut Ohio State's lead to 17-14. It would be the last touchdown of regulation.

The third quarter ended with Ohio State leading by three points and still alive in their chase of the ultimate dream. Miami had one quarter to try to come from three points down to extend their 34-game win streak and defend their title, which was very much in doubt.

Then Miami suffered a big loss. Just when it looked like running back Willis McGahee was getting his groove back, he went out with a serious knee injury. After catching a screen pass, McGahee moved up the right sideline to the Ohio State

40-yard line, and safety Will Allen delivered a hit that hyper-extended his knee. The tackle also stopped McGahee from getting the first down for Miami. So with more than 11 minutes to play, and down three points, the Hurricanes would have to go the rest of the way without one of their biggest weapons.

By keeping McGahee from getting the first down on the play in which he was injured, Ohio State forced Miami into a fourth-down decision. Kicker Todd Sievers was called on to try a 54-yard field goal for Miami, one yard longer than his longest of the season. The kick failed, and Ohio State took over at their own 37-yard line with 11 and a half minutes to play. It's hard to imagine there were any Buckeye fans who felt that three-point lead was safe. This was similar to situations that Ohio State found themselves in against Illinois and Michigan. But their inability to secure first downs and add additional points played a large part in those games going down to the final seconds.

The Buckeyes went to work, attempting to march down field. A first down to Miami's 39 occurred on a Krenzel-to-Gamble pass. All the while, the Buckeyes were trying to milk as much of the clock as they could. Clarett then chugged to the 28-yard line, moving the orange sticks again. Then all of a sudden it was third and 12. Krenzel then took off running to the Miami 25, stopped shy of the first down. So once again kicker Mike Nugent was called upon to attempt a 42-yarder. The sophomore from Centerville then experienced a rare miss. It was again up to the Ohio State defense to hold with six and a half minutes to play in the fourth quarter.

The task for Miami now was that much more challenging with McGahee out with the serious knee injury. If they were to have any success running the ball, they would have to turn to fullback Quatrine Hill, or Jarret Payton, the son of the late, great Walter Payton. Ken Dorsey once again turned to his best threat of the night, passing to tight end Winslow, and that combination got the 'Canes beyond midfield. Then Miami again seemed to be unable to handle success. Ken Dorsey hit Roscoe Parrish with a pass inside the OSU 20, but Parrish committed the fifth Hurricane turnover of the night when he fumbled the ball when hit by Donnie Nickey and Dustin Fox. safety Will Allen recovered it with five minutes-plus remaining, and the defense had again thrown water on Miami's fire.

Once again, though, the Ohio State offense was unable to put together a drive that would finish things off. Craig Krenzel continued to show his toughness, picking up a first down on a rush to the Buckeye 28-yard line. Down to three minutes to play in the fourth quarter, with Ohio State up by three points. An incompletion on third down to Chris Gamble, ruled out of bounds by the officials on a close call, brought about the need for another Andy Groom punt. His kick was fielded by Miami's Roscoe Parrish at the Hurricane 24, and for a few scary moments, it looked like all might be lost. Parrish flew up the right sideline past midfield and was eventually taken down by Groom at the Ohio State 26-yard line. Two minutes to play, and the Hurricanes had a chance.

The Ohio State defense would again be called upon to tough out another stand. Miami quarterback Ken Dorsey would once again feel the heat from the Buckeyes' front line.

Defensive end Simon Fraser would record a sack. Then a pass to Payton put the ball at the OSU 24-yard line with around 20 seconds to play. Miami would be given a chance to try to send this game into overtime. Todd Sievers, who earlier in the half was called on to try an improbable 54-yarder, would now try a 40-yarder to tie the game at 17. After all of the timeouts had been used, and with just three seconds on the clock, Sievers booted it through the uprights, sending college football's national title game for the first time ever into overtime.

Overtime Again

You'll recall the discussion on the Illinois game, how prior to it, Ohio State had never played an overtime game and that they were the last Big Ten team to ever take a contest beyond four quarters. Now for the second time in their last three games, they would have to log extra work to try to gain the biggest win since the accomplishments of the Super Sophomores in the 1969 Rose Bowl.

Those who had paid major dollars to travel to Arizona for this game had to feel like they had gotten more than their money's worth. They also had to be very hoarse at this point. Just an hour previously, when the Buckeyes had gone up by ten points, it looked like Ohio State might be ready to cruise away with a win. However, it was a tribute to Miami that they not only came from behind, but did so in a game in which they lost one of their biggest stars and had also turned the ball over five times.

Ohio State won the coin toss and, as per usual with the college overtime format, chose to be on defense first. Miami went right to their money connection. Ken Dorsey kept utilizing tight end Kellen Winslow and eventually hit him with a seven-yard touchdown pass. Sievers kicked the point after, and the burden was now on the Buckeyes to score seven to force a second overtime.

From the Miami 25-yard line, on Ohio State's OT possession, Craig Krenzel rushed to the 20-yard line. Then early movement by the offensive line cost OSU the five yards they had gained. The Buckeyes had been using a five-receiver alignment quite a bit and were doing so in overtime. Jamal Green then turned in a big defensive play for Miami by sacking Krenzel. Third and 14, ball at Miami's 29-yard line. Then an incomplete screen pass toward Clarett. Fourth down, 14 to go at Miami's 29, and the Buckeyes' dream of a national title rested on this one possibly final play.

Craig Krenzel looked to his money man, Michael Jenkins, and hit him on the right sideline to the Miami 12, getting the first down to continue the drive and the season. Everyone took a deep breath. On first down, Krenzel tossed an incompletion into the end zone, going for Jenkins again. Second down, 10 to go from the 12. Krenzel took off running to the five-yard line and took a big hit from Johnathan Vilma and Sean Taylor. This is probably where people started to realize the physical toughness that Krenzel brought to the table. After taking that hit, he bounced back up to get right to the business of the next play.

Third down at Miami's five-yard line. The Buckeyes needed three yards for the conversion. Krenzel, while scrambling, tossed into the end zone, where the ball was batted away from tight end Ben Hartsock by Sean Taylor.

Once again, fourth down. Once again, down to a possibly final play for Ohio State, who needed the first down, or a touchdown, plus PAT, to keep it going!

Fourth down, three to go, from the Miami five-yard line. From a shotgun formation and facing a blitz by the Hurricanes, Krenzel threw for the right corner of the end zone and Chris Gamble. The ball was batted away from Gamble by defensive back Glenn Sharpe. For a few quick seconds, it appeared that the game was over, that Miami had come from behind to defend their national title, that Ohio State's dreams had been crushed.

"There's a Flag! There's a Flag, A Late Flag! There's A Flag!" "He Got Mugged!"

The words of Jim Lachey boomed through our headphones after the pass was batted away from Gamble and a late flag was dropped by the officials. At this point, people had come running onto the field and the fireworks were being shot off at Sun Devil Stadium by those thinking that the game was over. Miami players were celebrating, and we were told that some of them had even started putting on ballcaps and T-shirts proclaiming the Hurricanes as champs again. But everyone waited for the call on the flag. It had to have been one of the fastest shifts in emotions that anyone in that stadium or listening to or watching this game had felt in their lives.

Initially, field judge Terry Porter ruled defensive holding against Glenn Sharpe of Miami, but then changed the call to pass interference. When asked why it took so long to toss the laundry, "I replayed it in my mind," said Porter. "I wanted to make double-sure that it was the right call." The call gave Ohio State a first down at Miami's two-yard line, keeping the dream alive. It was a call that would be talked about for weeks, even months after the game. The official in question said he saw the holding occur, thought about it for a second, then tossed the flag. Jim Lachey's comment on the matter probably summed up what every Buckeye fan was thinking. "He had a tough time getting it out of his pocket, but thank God he threw it."

So the overtime continued, and Ohio State still needed seven points to force a second overtime. On first and goal from the two, trailing 24-17, Maurice Clarett tried to run to the right side, and after running backwards was cut down by Miami at the one-yard line. Second and goal at the one. Once again, Clarett's number was called, and once again, Miami denied him. Third and goal at the one.

Not risking a handoff, Krenzel took it himself to the house! From one yard out, Craig Krenzel scored his second TD of the day, and the Buckeyes survived two fourth downs. They got a penalty that kept the game going. Now they needed an extra point to keep the game going.

The Buckeyes then created more problems for themselves. Movement on the line backed up the PAT try to the 15-yard line. Mike Nugent, atoning for his field goal miss in the second half, banged it through, tying the game at 24 all. The marathon would continue.

Overtime Number Two

Ohio State started the second overtime with the football. Runs by Lydell Ross and Maurice Clarett advanced the ball from the 25 to the 16. Then on third and one, Krenzel pushed it himself to the 11, getting a first down. Krenzel then completed a pass to Michael Jenkins that advanced the ball to the Miami five-yard line. Ohio State needed one more offensive play to stake their claim to a title.

It was Maurice Clarett from five yards out delivering the final offensive knockout, scoring his second touchdown of the game. Add in the point after by Mike Nugent, and Ohio State was up 31-24 and seemed to have asserted more physical domination on a Miami defense that, during this drive, was showing exhaustion.

Once again, it was up to the defense to preserve a win. The biggest win!

Miami got its chance to try to extend the game and push it to a third overtime, and the Buckeye defense took the field after getting a little respite, but was energized by the offensive score. On their first play of this overtime, running back Jarret Payton was thrown for a one-yard loss by Matt Wilhelm. On second down, Ken Dorsey tossed an incompletion for Kellen Winslow, but it was again Wilhelm making a big play. He breastboned the Hurricane quarterback, knocking him out of the game with a good, clean, solid hit. Dorsey had been taking a pounding from the Buckeye defense all night like he'd not seen all season.

He tried to get up after that hit, but was obviously woozy and left the field. Larry Coker was forced to send in his backup quarterback, sophomore Derek Crudup, with the title on the line. He had played in seven games, completing 25 passes and two TDs. Not an ideal spot for a guy to come into the game cold.

Crudup came in facing third and ten from OSU's 25. He completed a pass inside the 20 to Quadtrine Hill. It was now fourth and three at the Buckeye 18-yard line. Miami was in the position that Ohio State faced twice in the first overtime, needing a first down to keep the game going. The Buckeye defense faced an opportunity to end the game right here!

Miami called a timeout, and it gave Ken Dorsey a chance to return at quarterback.

Then Ohio State called a timeout to readjust to Dorsey's presence.

On fourth down, Dorsey completed a pass to Kellen Winslow, gaining the first down to the 11-yard line. But a facemask penalty against the Buckeyes gave Miami first and goal at the Buckeye six-yard line, continuing the drama.

With four cracks inside the ten, you had to like Miami's chances of making something happen. On first down, the Buckeyes were called for pass interference when Chris Gamble violated Andre Johnson, stopping what could have been a touchdown.

First down again, but from the OSU two-yard line. Jarret Payton then gained one yard, to the one. The Hurricanes were inching closer.

Second and goal from the OSU one-yard line. Dorsey then chucked an incompletion to their other tight end, Eric Winston.

Now third and goal from the OSU one-yard line. Fullback Quadtrine Hill was stopped shy of the goal line. One more strong stand for the Buckeye defense.

Once again, everything was down to one more play. A stop, and Ohio State would be national champs!

Fourth and goal for Miami at the OSU one-yard line. The Hurricanes brought in their pass personnel. Three wideouts and one set-back.

Dorsey dropped back to throw, and the Buckeyes were coming after him. Linebacker Cie Grant got to the Miami quarterback and made enough contact to alter his pass, which fell incomplete!

The marathon was over, the champions were de-throned, and Ohio State was the new king of the college football hill! The final score was 31-24 in two overtimes. It was what many people would call the best college game they ever saw. And the Buckeyes got a win over a team many thought they had no chance of beating—and in a game that, just a few moments before, it seemed they had lost.

This time when the fireworks went off and people stormed the field, it was for real. The Ohio State players and coaches were enjoying a moment that came in dreams.

They ended Miami's 34-game win streak and won the first title for Buckeye fans since 1968! It may have taken a while for it all to unfold, but the expressions were priceless.

"Wow," said Jim Lachey. "Can you believe it, I'm speechless with the way this team has fought. They've never made it easy, but they've never quit!"

"And from down the field, guys, for the first time this season, I have nothing more to say!" That was Jim Karsatos.

The sight and the sounds of Sun Devil Stadium were price-less. They would be replayed on TV, captured in photos and drilled in people's memories, never to be forgotten!

Championship Postgame

Once the game at Sun Devil Stadium ended and the spontaneous celebration of Buckeye players, coaches and fans had passed, the formalities began. From up in the press box, you saw stadium personnel moving a stage into place on the field, where the trophy presentation would occur. It was organized confusion to say the least, but while Buckeye players and coaches were being herded off to where they were supposed to be, the most obvious sight either on the field or in the stands was people in various forms of scarlet and gray garb jumping up and down and enjoying the moment.

Up in our booth, once the game ended, we still were looking back and forth at one another with a combination of shock and excitement, still not really grasping what we had just seen and broadcast for the last few hours.

Once the trophy was presented to Coach Tressel, he was to again utter a statement that, like others he has made, will ring in people's minds for years. "We are so proud of these young men, these 13 seniors. We've always had the best damn band in the land. Now we've got the best damn team in the land!"

To no surprise, quarterback Craig Krenzel was honored for his play in this game. While his passing numbers were 7-21 with 122 yards and two interceptions, his career-high 81 yards on the ground and two rushing scores showed the nation just how tough this Buckeye was. "It's no different than what we've done all year," Krenzel said. "We made plays when we had to."

The praises of Ohio State's defense would continue to be sung loud and clear after this championship game performance. Linebacker Robert Reynolds was among those basking in the glow of the title. "We had to take away their threats. Our D-line played their hearts out. We all played together, that's why we got so many turnovers.

"We knew as long as we could play one more play, we'd have a chance. We gave ourselves a chance to do that; it was awesome." This would cap off a truly special year for Reynolds and his family. His brother Pat played defensive end for the Western Kentucky football team, which won the NCAA 1-A title.

CHAPTER 5
NATIONAL CHAMPIONS

As the season progressed, and even into this championship game, there were those who doubted whether this Buckeye offense could survive so many close calls. Offensive lineman Shane Olivea typified the attitude shared by him and the rest of his mates with the ball. "We were supposed to have no chance in the world to win this game, that's why you play the games, and come to Ohio State, to play in games like this. I don't know how many more of these our fans can take, but they stuck with us. We weren't going to be intimidated at all. We made plays when we had to, truly a team effort. We just won the college football Super Bowl."

Most of what was occurring after the game involved the stage on the field where the trophy presentation was staged. Once Coach Tressel and a few selected players spoke at the stage, the championship trophy made its way around the platform where a number of the Buckeye players got their chance to spend quality time with that piece of hardware. One of the more memorable sights was linebacker Matt Wilhelm and defensive lineman Kenny Peterson holding that glass football between them and each planting a kiss on the prize!

Left Behind

There's no question that the Fiesta Bowl performance turned in by quarterback Craig Krenzel certified him as one tough hombre. That's something that Ohio State fans had become well aware of through the 2002 season, and maybe even Big Ten opponents could recognize the toughness of this young man, but those around the nation who followed college football maybe still weren't quite aware of what Krenzel brought to the table prior to January 3.

The way he gutted out the double-overtime thriller typified the intensity that Craig Krenzel played with, and it seemed to spread among his teammates. You've read all along about how in many of the games, when the offense seemed to be struggling, they kept the faith that something would eventually go their way, and that seemed to filter down from how Krenzel ran the huddle. So while he was honored for his play in the national championship game as the Offensive MVP, the postgame hubbub kept the junior signal caller more than busy with interviews, well-wishers, and celebrating. So much so that Krenzel missed the team bus back to the hotel.

There are reports that the football coaching staff, upon learning that their starting quarterback had been left behind, was going to send one of their police escort cars back to pick up Krenzel, but he was able to catch a ride with family. "I got a ride back with my parents," said Krenzel. "It was a long walk back to the car."

34-Year Wait

Not since the Rose Bowl in 1969, when Ohio State defeated Southern California, had the Buckeyes won a consensus championship. (In 1970, following a 9-1 ledger in '69 and a loss to Stanford in the Rose Bowl, OSU was declared the nation's top team by the National Football Foundation.) There had been many teams since the Super Sophomores of '68 that were felt to be serious contenders for the top prize, but it took 34 years to bridge the generations of champions. During the course of the 2002 season, numerous comparisons were made to the 1968 bunch.

Hours earlier, prior to kickoff for the Fiesta Bowl, the '68 champs were noted in the locker room. In a story later related by Jim Tressel, he explained that a '68 team photo was brought to the current-day players in Tempe. Along with player signatures, the photo contained the inscription, "We're all behind you! Go do it!"

Just like on this night in 2003 in Tempe, those Buckeyes in '68 were led by a sturdy, tough-nosed quarterback who typified leadership when in the huddle. The pride of Lancaster, Ohio, Rex Kern, like the rest of his teammates, held a special place in the lore of Ohio State football. It was on this night of the Fiesta in Arizona that Kern got to witness the past and the present come together and got to share his feelings on the radio with us.

"It's a great moment, a moment these guys will live the rest of their lives. These kids have captured the hearts of all Buckeye fans because of how they won the game and the way they won each and every game this season. They were incredible."

Kern also didn't mind admitting that the events of the night brought tears to his eyes. "The old man [Woody Hayes] would be happy because they go into the shotgun, and ran the quarterback off-tackle. The old man would have loved that."

Then when Kern was asked if Ohio State should continue recruiting redheaded quarterbacks (like Krenzel and himself) he replied, "Make sure they keep their hair for a long time."

Another of those from the '68 championship team who enjoyed the moment from afar was Larry Zelina, a wingback on that last title club. While he was able to send his son to the Fiesta Bowl, Larry was, like many, watching each and every anxious moment from home in Columbus. "There were a lot of similarities in the two teams, winning big games by close scores and overachieving a little."

As far as that memorable night this past January, Zelina remarked, "It was as incredible a game as I've ever seen, long overdue! The mystique of the '68 team was embellished any time an Ohio State team got close. It's a great feeling to pass the torch; it should have happened other times before."

I must admit that I am old enough to have vague memories of that team in 1968 and, as an 11-year-old kid, to have realized that they commanded high regard. It is amazing when you think of some of the teams that many thought could reach this goal, but one that came in with so little fanfare made such a big bang!

The Phone Calls

It may have been one of the longest postgame radio shows that I had ever been involved in, but with good reason. It's not often that you get to call and witness a national title game that falls the way of the team you're broadcasting for. By the time we finished up our on-the-air responsibilities, it may have been an hour and a half to two hours after the game was over. If memory serves me correct, it was at least 1:00 a.m., eastern time.

Once we were done and got out of the booth so that postgame audio could be shipped back to the station in Columbus and the equipment could be broken down, the realization of how big an accomplishment this was hit me.

I had nearly 20 messages on my cell phone from family and friends about Ohio State winning the national championship and their excitement over the game.

The most notable call came from my mother, who lives in retirement now in Henderson, Nevada. She is an Ohio State graduate and grew up in Columbus. To say she was thrilled is an understatement.

Another of the calls came from Wisconsin broadcaster Matt Lepay. He and his wife, Linda, both native Ohioans, called to express their congratulations. There were calls from friends from the Columbus area, some back home, some in Arizona, just caught up in the moment. Many of those calls I couldn't understand because of the noise factor.

There were calls from friends in my hometown of Cincinnati. One buddy of mine, Randy Johnston, called first, right at the start of overtime, then at the end of the game. The first call was easier to decipher than the second.

There was even a call from a friend in Florida, Maggie Erne, who did a fair amount of her growing up in Ohio. She relayed the story of watching the game in a Ft. Myers sports bar, and that some Miami fans were asking her, "Are those marijuana leaves on the side of the Ohio State helmets?" (Referring to the Buckeye leaves given to players for big plays.) They probably wouldn't have asked her that if they knew she was in law enforcement!

It was just another indication of how big a deal this was to Buckeye fans all over!

Eruption Back Home

While Tempe, Arizona was exploding with enthusiasm over Ohio State upsetting Miami and winning the national championship, Buckeye fans all across the country were busting loose with their celebrations over this dramatic game, topping off such a wild season.

At the aforementioned Buckeye Hall of Fame Cafe, the night was one to remember for those in attendance. Alyssa Skoczen is a regular bartender there and says one of the craziest nights she ever worked there turned out to be one of the most enjoyable.

"Obviously it was a zoo, really busy, the placed was filled to the brim! From the fourth quarter through both overtimes, all the people in the bar wanted us to enjoy the game like they were. We came from our side of the bar and watched it with the customers. Then during commercials, we made laps all around the place serving drinks, until the game started again."

Once the game ended, Alyssa explained that it was as crazy as you might have expected.

"I couldn't have thought of any place else I would have wanted to be working at that night!"

Hockey Team Turned Football Fans

On the night Ohio State was playing and beating Miami in the Fiesta Bowl, the NHL's Columbus Blue Jackets were playing in Washington D.C. against the Capitals. That game ended in a 2-2 tie, but while the staff and players were involved in that game with the Caps, many were trying as best they could to keep up with what was going on in Tempe that same night.

Among them was Jason Rothwell, assistant director of communications, who said that while watching the Blue Jackets and Caps from the MCI Center, they were able to occasionally check out the Fiesta Bowl from a press box TV. "Once our game went into overtime, I went down to the locker room, waiting for whenever it ended for the players to come off the ice, and there was a TV on in the locker room where I was able to keep up with the football game," said Rothwell, an Ohio State graduate.

The Blue Jackets-Capitals game ended right about the time the Fiesta Bowl went to halftime. Once the Jackets boarded their bus to go from the MCI Center to Dulles airport, they followed a majority of the second half while listening to the ESPN radio national broadcast. Still anxious to keep track of things once boarding the team's private jet, Rothwell immediately grabbed the jump-seat right behind the cockpit, so that he could attempt to continue listening on the radio. "I asked if anyone was going to sit in the jumpseat," said Rothwell, "and when they said no, I said there is now!"

As the Blue Jackets' aircraft was taxiing for takeoff in Virginia, Jason said he could hear Miami's final drive that led to the Hurricane field goal that tied the game and forced over-time.

"From there, most of what I could hear was scratchy and full of static. There was a little bit of a gap, but after a while we could pick up pieces of the local broadcast." (WBNS Radio.)

While listening to what he could hear from both overtimes, Jason would relay what happened to the pilot and copilot, and they would then describe what was happened over the jet's loudspeaker to the rest of the traveling party. While the signal again was crackling bad, Jason says he could hear the controversial fourth-down play in the first overtime when Chris Gamble was unable to catch a pass in the end zone, seemingly ending the game and winning it for Miami. "They didn't get it," was what Jason relayed to the pilot, but then upon hearing Jim Lachey yell, "He got mugged," Jason yelled to the pilot, "Hold on, there may be a flag!" He was then able to pass along the news that the game would continue and eventually move to a second extra frame.

"During the second overtime, the signal came in clear," said Jason. They were on their final approach to Port Columbus Airport when the Fiesta Bowl ended, and he was able to begin the chain of communication to the rest of the Blue Jacket organization on board that Ohio State had won the national title. "We could even see fireworks going off over different parts of town when the jet was landing!"

Another Ohio State graduate who was hoping after the hockey game to follow the Fiesta Bowl was Blue Jackets radio analyst Bill Davidge, who also got prompted along by one of the players. "After the game, when we got on the bus, Marc Denis [Columbus goaltender] came up and asked me if we could get the bus driver to turn the game on radio. Along with Dave King [head coach] we got him to turn it on," said Davidge. Then as they listened to the updates of the game being relayed through Rothwell, by way of the pilots on the loudspeaker, Bill explained when they became aware of the final outcome, "The plane went nuts! It was great! And being an ex-Buckeye, it means a lot!"

Championship Hangover

Not that anyone was in a hurry for the feeling to end, but it finally came time to leave Sun Devil Stadium and head back to the Scottsdale Hotel, which would be home for just a few more hours. It seemed almost like a day ago when we got to the stadium, and it was a thrilling but exhausting feeling to have witnessed this truly classic game. The same could be said for this amazing season of 2002.

Quite honestly, the top items on the agenda were change clothes, open a cold beer, dip into Jim Karsatos's supply of good cigars, sit in an overstuffed chair, maybe put my feet on a coffee table, and most importantly, toast the Buckeyes. By the time we got back, the hotel and surrounding areas were abuzz with celebration. Every now and then, you'd hear a roar from near the front of the hotel. Had to figure it was player(s) making their way back to home base and being greeted by the loyal following.

Our post-stadium cast party moved to the room occupied by D.R. Railsback. Did I say room? Excuse me. It was a suite! When D.R. checked into the hotel the day before the game, he got stranded at the front desk for about 15 minutes before they got his reservation straightened out. I'm thinking the hotel goofed up his reservation. To make up for that, they placed him in a very nice two-room suite, which was where we gathered upon returning from the game. As time went on, the gathering grew. Not only did it include our radio group, and various family and friends, it opened up to include university staff members, former Ohio State teammates of both Karsatos and Lachey, and some unknowns. A lot of this had to do with the fact that the watering holes in the hotel shut down early, or that the prices for adult beverages were sky high!

Among the unknowns, former Cleveland Indians pitcher Charles Nagy wandered in and got introduced around, much to the delight of some of the Tribe fans among us. It truly was a unique night. People were still wandering around somewhat in a daze over the game they had just witnessed and that Ohio State had actually managed to hang on and win the title, just like they had won so many games during the 2002 season. You just wondered when it was really going to sink in.

It wasn't really what you might consider a party, but more just relaxing and winding down. With the length of the game and how long it took to take care of all the things that needed to be done at the stadium, the little time we had to enjoy had gotten away. At one point I remember looking at my watch, and there were only two hours left until it was time to leave the hotel for the airport and the flight home.

Two hours later, there we were, checking out of the hotel while some of the Buckeye revelers were still celebrating the title. While the Valley of the Sun was still dark, we trotted sleepily off to Sky Harbor International Airport in Phoenix for the journey home. Not that it helped any, but the airport was full of Buckeye fans heading back home who appeared to be just as tired and sleepy. But even through the weariness, you could still feel the excitement that was generated by that amazing night at Sun Devil Stadium. Travelers wore their Ohio State hats, T-shirts, and sweatshirts with pride. They had seen the most exciting sporting event that many had ever witnessed, and they might be bone-tired, but they had been there in person to be a part of the Buckeye championship. Once again the additional airport security made getting checked in a marathon process and added to the time and exhaustion, but there still was an air of enthusiasm.

While at the airport, and before departure, the rumble of the stomach let it be known that food was required before the long trip home. Upon walking into one of the airport eateries, I sat down with Jim and Susan Karsatos, who had already begun feasting. After ordering, I began listening in on the conversation Jim was having with our waitress at the counter.

After working the past several days at the airport during the Fiesta Bowl stretch, she wanted to know a couple of things. First off, she wanted to know if anyone was left in Ohio. It seemed to her that everyone who resided in the Buckeye state must have become a snowbird for the week and fled to Arizona. Secondly, she wanted to know how the bars stayed in business in Ohio. We weren't quite sure what she meant, at first. She explained that while working during the past few days, the watering holes in the airport, and other places around the Phoenix area ran out of certain beers. Since the game was on a Friday, most establishments couldn't replenish their beer supplies until the following Monday, so it put them in a tough spot. Gives us a great deal to be proud of, right?

Eventually it came time to begin the long trek home, and it seemed that most of the people were headed either back to Ohio or various other points of origin. What most everyone seemed to have in common is that they were thrilled to have witnessed this remarkable title game, and that because of the flat-out exhaustion, all were anxious to get home.

The day was a strange one for me, because I missed an Ohio State basketball game that day with Louisville in Columbus. While making flight connections in Minneapolis, I became aware that the Buckeyes had let a good-sized lead get away and that the game was going into overtime. Ohio State eventually lost. It just seemed strange to miss the game, even thought it was for the Fiesta Bowl. It was only the second time I had missed a game for Ohio State (first was after being unable to get from the Sugar Bowl in New Orleans to Madison, Wisconsin for a hoops game due to a snowstorm).

It was a relief to finally get back home on the night of January 4, but it was also a time to ponder just what had occurred in the last 24 hours and how things would be different. Once home and assuming the position on the living room couch, I made a very weak attempt at watching the NFL playoff game between Atlanta and Green Bay. I remember seeing the first series or two, and the next thing I knew, they were interviewing Michael Vick on TV after the Falcons had won the game.

Valley of the Sun Cashes In

Once January 3 came and went, most Ohio State Buckeye fans were concerning themselves with getting back home and trying to enjoy the title as much as possible. Buying championship items like T-shirts, hats, etc., seemed to be on people's minds. Others were concerned with watching replays of the Fiesta Bowl telecasts. I and those I work with were deluged with questions about when our radio station might re-broadcast the game on radio and how people could get tapes of the game.

While everyone back in Ohio was doing their own reminiscing about the fantastic championship ride provided by the Buckeyes, the people back in Arizona were enjoying a financial windfall as a result of the Fiesta Bowl and the strong turnout by Ohio State fans. According to a story in the *Buckeye Sports Bulletin*, the championship game itself provided $153.7 million for the Phoenix metropolitan area. Those figures were collected in a survey by the sports business program at Arizona State University. These numbers exceeded the previous Fiesta Bowl best, which was set in the 1999 championship game, also staged at Sun Devil Stadium, between Tennessee and Florida State, which brought in over $133 million.

The survey further broke down some of the numbers, citing a record number of over 90,000 out-of-state visitors responsible for more than $91 million spent on food, hotels, and various other entertainment and connected purchases in the Phoenix area.

Memorabilia Galore

While the Phoenix area seemed to have hit a big payday, once you got back in Ohio, you couldn't turn anywhere without seeing a glut of Fiesta Bowl and national championship merchandise. Sporting goods stores, groceries, pharmacies, and street-side vendors were hawking everything and anything you could imagine that had enough space to print Ohio State, National Champions. The prices certainly showed that someone was going to profit from the Buckeyes' title, although to be fair, some of those prices did come down a little as time went on. Copies of the front page of the *Columbus Dispatch* on the morning after the Fiesta Bowl became hot items.

I added to my memorabilia collection and purchased a framed photograph of the final play of the Fiesta Bowl, which hangs proudly in my sports room in the lower level of my house on a wall that includes my press pass from the game, the front page of the final stat sheet, and the front page of the *Arizona Republic* from the morning after the game.

Celebration in the Cold

Not long after the Fiesta Bowl was over and people began the task of resuming their normal lives, the question cropped up about a ceremony to honor the national champions in Columbus. One of the immediate obstacles that kept things from happening right away was the NCAA Coaches Convention that Jim Tressel would be attending. There was the other matter of recruiting.

Then it was announced that on Saturday afternoon, January 18, the Buckeye football team would assemble in Ohio Stadium for fans to honor, and the championship trophy would be on hand. Admission would be free, and the event would be broadcast live both on radio and television. Scheduling worked out from the standpoint that the basketball team was playing at home that evening against Wisconsin, so there would be no direct conflict with another big-revenue sporting event on campus.

It was on that Saturday morning that I drove to the Value City Arena for the basketball team's game-day shootaround, a normal ritual to acquire a pregame interview with basketball coach Jim O'Brien. It's also important to point out that it was cold, very cold, that day. Maybe 20 degrees at the most.

Despite the frigid outlook, that morning there were people parked in lots around the campus and stadium as if it were a regular game day Saturday morning, with barbeque grills, lawn chairs, coolers, and all the other accessories you would see in the fall. Folks were coming from all around the state to pay homage to the national champions. There were estimates that between 20,000 and 50,000 people braved these elements to get one more glimpse of the team that captured everyone's hearts with their thrilling march to the title. A true testament to Buckeye fans! An estimated 60,000 Buckeye fans braved the frigid elements to soak up more of the champions.

Presidential Visit and the Great Snow Angel Caper

It's a usual occurrence for teams that win major sports championships to making the traditional visit to Washington D.C. and to get an audience with the president at the White House. This trip was eventually arranged for the Ohio State Buckeyes for Monday, February 24. The Buckeyes were one of four college sports teams to get a chance to spend time with President Bush.

President Bush had visited the Ohio State campus the previous spring for graduation. The President relayed the comments made to him in the spring by Jim Tressel. "He said, 'Watch us this year, we're gonna be pretty good, and we may be visiting you in the White House.'"

Upon greeting Ohio State and the other athletic teams, President Bush did manage to get a chuckle from the assembled masses when he commented, "For some reason, it seems like we have a large contingent from the state of Ohio."

When the Ohio State football team visited the White House, there was mischief underfoot, and the guilty culprit was tight end Ben Hartsock. After the presidential visit and the formalities, word circulated back to Columbus that Ben Hartsock had run afoul of the Secret Service.

Hartsock relayed the story later that day in an interview on WBNS-AM, in Columbus, that he and quarterback Craig Krenzel were walking on the grounds when he wondered if anyone had ever made a snow angel on the White House lawn. Hartsock then explained what happened as he prepared to make history and started to put one foot on the lawn. "Secret Service agents were yelling at me, and needless to say, I stopped. I imagined six different cross-hairs aimed at me." Hartsock also added, "Nobody else had done it, and we wanted to leave our mark."

The young man from Chillicothe, Ohio, also added that during the trip he noticed that "they didn't have a doorbell on the front door of the White House." Then he concluded by saying, "I think I left my mark on the White House and am probably banished!"

Championship Rings

If you get into this business of being around sports, after a while you'll come across people who have championship rings from one sport or another. They may be former players, like one of my partners, Jim Lachey, who has a Super Bowl ring from his playing days with the Washington Redskins. Or they may be other media types who have covered teams that won titles. In the college field, even if the radio announcers don't work directly for the school, but are still involved in broadcasting their games, the announcers generally are given championship rings, or given the opportunity to purchase them.

Maybe an hour after the Fiesta Bowl game between Ohio State and Miami was over, one of my co-workers, Ian Fitzsimmons, was in our radio booth. He made the comment to Jim Lachey, Jim Karsatos and me, "You guys should get championship rings, right?" I must admit the question caught me off guard. It wasn't something I had thought about. I didn't think about it that much after Ian had asked the question until I ran into some of the other radio announcers in the Big Ten during basketball season. Guys like Steve Jones and Penn State and Matt Lepay at Wisconsin and Gary Dolphin at Iowa were offering me congratulations (as if I made one single play) and saying that they were happy for me since I should be getting a championship ring. As nice as it was that all of these people asked about it, my reply was always, "Well, I don't know if we get one or not."

I must admit that while I hadn't thought about it much before, all of the questions about it had me wondering and hoping that maybe we would be given the chance to purchase the rings. I have friends who own championship rings from when the Cincinnati Reds won World Series titles in 1975, '76, and '90, and I can tell the importance those items have to them. I have been involved in the past with Bengals games with both Dave Lapham and Anthony Munoz and have seen the rings they each received for Cincinnati's appearances in the Super Bowl. Jim Lachey very proudly sports a ring he got from playing on a Washington Redskins Super Bowl championship team. So the question raised a great deal of interest.

Then the call came from Jim Lachey. The two of us and Jim Karsatos had been summoned to the equipment manager's office at the football complex to get sized for championship rings. The day we went over was Valentine's Day, 2003, and I was preparing to leave for Ann Arbor and an Ohio State basketball game with the University of Michigan. I hadn't been sized for a right-hand ring since high school, but it really was a special moment.

Please don't even begin to think that me, my partners, or other university employees who are given this special privilege feel anywhere near as deserving of the honor as the players and coaches who are responsible for this national title. It is, however, a great gesture on the part of the university to show how important their relationship with our company is and that they feel their three radio announcers should be included. The players and coaches actually were to receive two rings each. The first set was given to just the players, coaches and football staff. The second set, which was also going to be made available to members of the athletic department, was what we would receive.

On that day in February when I went to the equipment office to get sized, I didn't even get to see the artwork on what the rings would look like. That was a question everyone kept asking. "What will they look like?" I couldn't provide any kind of answer.

Then on June 26, Jim Lachey called me. He had gone to the Woody Hayes Football Complex the day before to pick up his ring, and collected mine as well. Jim and his wife, Ann, delivered mine to our radio station. It was a breathtaking sight to first open the gift box and see the ring itself. On one side, it has the score of the Ohio State-Michigan game, 14-9, along with my last name. On the other side panel, it says Ohio State, Perfect Season, 14-0. It also has a block "O" and the score of the Fiesta Bowl win over Miami, 31-24. On top there is a red stone that contains the number one, which has diamonds inside the number, and around the stone it says National Champions, Big Ten Champions, and Fiesta Bowl.

I must admit to not being much of a jewelry person, but this will be a very prized possession, and I will own and wear it with great memories of the 2002 season.

Tribute to Bert Charles

This past winter, while all were enjoying the afterglow of Ohio State's national championship, a familiar face and voice connected to Buckeye football was lost. Bert Charles passed away during the winter months after a lengthy illness. Bert spent 33 years calling Ohio State games on the radio, with his last game a Buckeye win over Michigan in Ann Arbor in 1981. That day, Art Schilchter rushed for two touchdowns.

I first met Bert during the 2000 season when I recorded an interview with him to be played prior to an Ohio State-Illinois game in Champaign. I never had the pleasure of hearing Bert's broadcasts live. While growing up and spending most of my life in Cincinnati, we heard the Buckeye games broadcast by outlets other than his station. In those days, it wasn't uncommon for schools to give more than one broadcast outlet. It occurred for years both with Michigan and Iowa. In recent years I have been able to listen to tapes of the games Bert did, with our station rebroadcasting memorable Ohio State football games to get folks in the mood for football in the months leading up to the start of a season. There's no question that this man had great excitement and enthusiasm for the games he witnessed, such as the '68 win for Ohio State over number-one Purdue, and countless battles with archrival Michigan. Very recently I had a chance to hear Bert call the controversial Ohio State loss at Michigan State in 1974. His voice and his passion for the game made for great theatre of the ear.

My association with Bert was nowhere near as long or as detailed as it must have been for many others. But you could always count on a firm handshake, a genuine smile, and sincere compliments and best wishes. His spirit and demeanor were still upbeat even when fighting the illness that eventually took him. Bert attended the weekly press luncheons for the football coaches. He worked in the press box on home game days and provided telephone updates for out-of-market radio stations. Often, Bert would come into our booth prior to the games, and since the rest of the press box was enclosed with windows that could not open, Bert would always very politely ask if he could listen to the entrance of the Ohio State Marching Band in our booth. Sometimes he would, and other times he listened somewhere else.

Bert's daughter, Meridith Trapp, was kind enough to share some of her memories of her father and how his last season following Ohio State and the 2002 national championship season brought great joy to him. "He was my hero, and I was such a tomboy. Because of the unusual and late hours he would work, he bought a white football and would toss it with me at night." While Bert worked all the home games, Meridith said he would watch all of he road games with a legal pad and pen, chart all of the plays, and prepare himself for the next Monday's press conference and any questions he might ask. She said even on the night of the Fiesta Bowl, he was stationed in front of the TV, taking notes.

When it came time to deliver a eulogy at her father's funeral, Meridith made sure that his association and appreciation for Ohio State and his days watching Buckeye football got their proper due. "He had an undying zeal for Ohio State football and game-day Saturdays. We could ask for no greater gift than to have given him in his final months that wholly thrilling season and national championship of 2002." Another touch that was not lost on the family was the attendance at the funeral of former Ohio State head coach John Cooper.

Someone who had cultivated a regular relationship with Bert in the last few years was a fellow employee, Eric Kaelin of WBNS-AM. Eric would gather some of Bert's old tapes for rebroadcasts of games and would take the time to just socialize with him. When talking about first meeting Bert, Eric relayed, "When I first went to attend one of Coach Cooper's Media Lunches, I was lost and didn't know what to do. Bert and Marv Homan, [former sports information director and fellow announcer] urged me to sit with them, saying, 'Come sit with us old guys.'" Eric said the benefit was all his. "He was a world of knowledge."

Eric also said that Bert's continued involvement on game days by working in the Ohio State press box had great importance in this man's life.

"Just being part of something he had been part of for so long and continuing in any capacity was therapy for him. He lived Ohio State." In December, when Bert was not in the best of health, Eric took the time to have lunch with Bert at one of his favorite haunts, a local Chinese restaurant.

"He was thinner, and weak, but still was concerned about me," said Eric, "and was full of —— and vinegar, talking about

Buckeyes. He thought they had good chance of beating Miami." And in his last reflection of Bert, Eric said, "Two of his favorite things were Chinese food and martinis. We both had Chinese, and while Bert couldn't have the martini, I had one for him."

Here's to you, Bert!

Showing for the Public

On April 9, of 2003, the annual Ohio State Spring Football Preview event was staged at the Woody Hayes Complex. It's an event that is tied in with the local Alzheimer's Association, began a number of years ago by former head coach John Cooper. It was an event to bring awareness to the fight against Alzheimer's started by Coach Cooper, whose mother-in-law battled the disease. When Jim Tressel became head coach at Ohio State, he sought out advice and thoughts from his predecessor on certain areas involving the job. As Tressel would relay during his first Spring Preview, Coach Cooper had asked that he see his way clear to continue this Spring Preview event, a request that Coach Tressel gladly acted on.

The main purpose of this event, from a fan standpoint, was to hear comments from the Ohio State head coach and to get a little briefing on where the team stood regarding spring practice. This would be one of the first public appearances by the football program en masse, after the National Championship. You can imagine that the public hunger for any part of this football program was gigantic, and the turnout for this event showed evidence of that. Also, in a typical classy move by Jim Tressel, as he had done the year before, he invited coach

John Cooper and his wife Helen to be part of the event and sit at the head table. Also seated at the head table was Coach Cooper's predecessor, Earle Bruce. Coach Bruce had been inducted into the College Football Hall of Fame during the 2002 championship season. It was also Coach Bruce who had employed Jim Tressel as an assistant at Ohio State in the 1980s. What you had at this event were all three men who had served as head coaches of the Buckeye football program since Woody Hayes. As I think back to seeing all three of these gentlemen sitting together at the head table for this spring preview, it made you gain a greater appreciation for the strength of the Ohio State football tradition.

One of the other great touches to this event was the recognition given to numerous members of the 1968 national championship Ohio State Buckeyes. This was a group that had always been held in high regard as the last Buckeye team to claim the top prize. They held a mystique and a special place in the minds and hearts of Buckeyes fans because they were the last national champs. They no longer were the most recent national champs. Now with the achievements of the 2002 team, it seemed fitting that a group that for over 30 years carried the banner of the last champions were paid tribute while all were still basking in the glow of the current championship.

Spring Game

When any football team begins spring practice, it provides a sneak peek for followers of things maybe to come for the following fall. You can only imagine the anticipation of spring drills in 2003 for the national champion Buckeyes. With all of the off-season attention and appearance requests, the coaching staff made a decision to limit public access to spring practices, which added to the anticipation of the April 26 Scarlet and Gray spring scrimmage.

As the annual spring game approached and fans were anxious to get their first look on the field at the Buckeyes since that memorable night of January 3 in Tempe, head coach Jim Tressel talked in his radio pregame interview about the importance of putting the national title in its proper perspective and in the past. "We needed to move along right after the Fiesta Bowl. It's human nature to admire your work, but in college football you don't have time," said Tressel. "Our guys and our coaches have done a good job of that. I've liked the spirit everyone's had in the spring."

One of the things the Ohio State coach hoped would emerge in the spring of 2003 was leadership, something that was a crucial part of the 2002 team's success.

"With a number of seniors, more than 20, it will be interesting to see leaders emerging." We won't see who they will be until adverse situations occur." Tressel also talked about carrying the national title making the targets on their backs that much larger. "The bar has been moved even higher than it normally is."

As the excitement of the spring game approached, even Andy Geiger, the director of athletics, warned about a lingering championship hangover while speaking in a halftime interview. "You worry about that a little," said Geiger, "because focus is how you win championships. It was the greatest moment in all of our lives, or close to it, but August 30 we play the University of Washington Huskies, who mean to put themselves in harm's way. They aim to stop our streak and get a streak of their own going, and it becomes serious business in its own way." But Geiger also didn't want to curb the enthusiasm about the spring game, saying, " It's time to take a spring drink from the Buckeye football water, if you will."

Despite the official urgings to move beyond the championship season and focus on the next campaign, it was a day for Buckeye fans to enjoy themselves. More than 50,000 fans paid the five-dollar ticket price and enjoyed themselves in a 37-29 win by the Scarlet team over the Gray. Another notable segment of the spring game was the involvement of many former Ohio State players in the day's festivities. Dozens who, in the past, had played for Ohio State roamed the sidelines, serving as honorary coaches and just mingling with the current-day players. Joey Galloway, former Buckeye wide receiver who is currently employed by the Dallas Cowboys, presented the university with a $100,000 check to establish the Galloway Family Athletic Scholarship Fund. It's aimed at helping athletes from Galloway's Ohio Valley home area who attend Ohio State.

In a radio interview on WBNS-AM during the week leading up to the spring game, Galloway said, "I was trying to think of a way to help out Ohio State and help out a young person from my area, and that's the best way to do it."

The other plus to the day was the fact that somewhere in the neighborhood of 20 high school football prospects from within the state of Ohio were on hand to watch the spring game and get just a little taste of what a game day at Ohio Stadium might be like.

Reward

It didn't take too long after the Fiesta Bowl and Ohio State's national championship for people to begin wondering if head coach Jim Tressel might be in line for a contract extension. There had been some precedence at Ohio State regarding such a matter, with Jim O'Brien having been so rewarded after the basketball Buckeyes made the Final Four in 1999. Tressel's original deal was set to expire following the 2005 season. The Buckeye coach even admitted in an article in the *Columbus Dispatch* that getting the Ohio State position was about the job, not the finances. "When I interviewed here, I didn't even ask what they paid, that wasn't why I wanted to come here."

On June 16, 2003, Jim Tressel's reward arrived. The school announced a new six-year deal for the coach that would run through the 2008 season. It was an agreement that could be extended for three years if agreed upon by March 1, 2006. It was also a deal that would pay over 1.3 million dollars in year one and over 1.8 million in year six. The package also included deferred compensation, as well as an estimated $100,000 annually in academic bonuses. At the request of Tressel, the only athletic bonus is tied to Ohio State's participation in the Bowl Championship Series championship game. Should that once again occur, the cash register hits again for $200,000.

"I want to thank President [Karen] Holbrook, Andy Geiger [Director of Athletics] and the board of trustees for their support and belief in me," said Tressel on the day the package was announced. "Ellen [his wife] and I look forward to spending at least the next six years here and working hard to accomplish the goals that we have set for ourselves and our student athletes." In typical Tressel fashion, he was quick to give credit to others. "I know, too, that any success we have had here is due in large part to the hard work and support of the people around me, particularly my coaching staff, our players, the entire administration and support staff and, of course, every single Ohio State Buckeye fan. They have my sincere thanks. I am truly humbled to be a small part of the Ohio State University, because I believe this is one of the great institutions of higher learning in this country."

When offering his comments on the matter, athletic director Andy Geiger said basically the decision was a slam dunk. "I am absolutely elated with this agreement," said Geiger. "Certainly it is an appropriate reward for what Coach Tressel has already accomplished on and off the field. Jim is an outstanding coach and teacher, as well as a tremendous person. His services to the University and the state of Ohio speak volumes as to the type of person he is and his core values. Ohio State football could not be in better hands."

In massive agreement with Geiger was university president Karen Holbrook. "Coach Tressel is doing a truly outstanding job in his work with the players and staff, and also as a university ambassador. He is committed to excellence and values that reflect the highest standards and integrity. Jim is an asset to Ohio State, and I am pleased that we have reached an agreement that will keep him here for the foreseeable future."

Also, in typical Tressel fashion, one of his first concerns in getting this new contract hammered out was to make sure that his assistant coaches were taken care of.

Championship Reflections

One of the questions that has been a constant since the conclusion of the Fiesta Bowl is, "What was it like?" While I've been asked numerous times, just imagine the players and coaches from the 2002 Buckeyes and how often they've been barraged with it.

It's been interesting to hear various versions of what this season meant to different people. For me, to see how it affected the two guys I worked closely with during the year, Jim Karsatos and Jim Lachey, was truly enjoyable. These are two guys who had a great deal of athletic success in their younger years as players at Ohio State, Big Ten championships, bowl games, and in Jim Lachey's case, a Super Bowl title with the Washington Redskins. But they were like kids soaking up every bit of the success of 2002.

Another guy I sought out was Jerry Rudzinski, former linebacker and co-captain with the Ohio State teams in the late 1990s. As a matter of fact, Jerry was a co-captain of the '98 team that spent most of the regular season ranked number one in the nation. Jerry said that when the season began, while not being ready to predict a national title, he thought the 2002 Buckeyes might have the ingredients of a successful ball club. "With their home schedule [eight games] a solid defense, and Krenzel playing mistake-free football, I thought they could get over the top."

As most people looked at the Buckeyes' matchup with Miami in the Fiesta Bowl as a daunting task, there was a moment in which Jerry felt this Ohio State team maybe had a chance very few outside the team ranks gave them. "I remember during pregame warms ups, sitting in the top row of Sun Devil Stadium, and watching the defense. When I looked at each of those starting 11 players on defense, I saw NFL-type potential," said Rudzinksi. "It didn't matter how explosive Miami was on offense; I thought because of that defense, Ohio State had a chance to win that game."

Once the second overtime was concluded, Jerry found himself, like many other former players and even more Ohio State fans, reveling in the moment. "I thought about those seniors, their last go-round, the biggest three to four months of their lives. These seniors had been on a roller-coaster ride during their careers, a 6-6 season that ended without a bowl game and a head coaching change. It couldn't have been easy to take."

You would think it would be human nature for former players to think what it would have been like had their teams been able to enjoy the moment that this team enjoyed in Tempe, Arizona, and Rudzinski certainly could be excused for that when you consider how close some of the teams he played on in the late 1990s came. "Some seasons, we didn't make the big play when we needed it, couldn't get over the top, but every time this team faced one of those situations, they did it."

For those of you who don't know Jerry Rudzinski, he personifies the class that is Ohio State and its football program. As a matter of fact, when I first came to Columbus, Jerry was one of the first players I ever interviewed, and even as a student athlete, he carried himself in a respectful and team-oriented manner. Also at the conclusion of the championship, his thoughts turned to former teammates. There were a handful of fifth-year seniors on this championship team who were redshirt freshmen when Jerry was playing his final season as a Buckeye in 1998. "I thought of guys like Donnie Nickey, David Thompson, and Cie Grant. They started number one [when Ohio State was the preseason top team in the nation] and ended number one. What they did put pride in me, made me proud to be part of a tradition that produced a national championship."

Among others offering their look back at 2002, Marla Ridenour of the *Akron Beacon-Journal* cites developments in September that set the tone for the championship run. "From a heart-rate perspective, the Cincinnati game was the most stressful," said Marla. "I was a basket case. Also I felt going into the Fiesta Bowl that they had proved something, whether they had won or not."

Also through her work covering the Cleveland Browns, Marla relayed comments from Butch Davis, the Browns' head coach who had recruited many of the Hurricane players on the 2002 team. "He thought the key play in the game was Michael Jenkins's catch on fourth down in the first overtime, which kept the game going. He thought if Miami stops that play, then the controversial play [involving Chris Gamble and Glenn Sharpe in the end zone with official Terry Porter] never happens."

Another to chip in with his thought on the Buckeyes' championship was Chris Spielman, one of the greatest linebackers ever to don the Scarlet and Gray. A two-time All-American and three-time All-Big Ten performer, his career was highlighted with the 1987 Lombardi Award, and he stands as the school leader in career solo tackles. Chris set a standard that remains untouched in dedication and intensity.

"It's been my belief that the tradition and honor at Ohio State has long been set before me and will be long set after me," said Speilman. "Watching the guys win the national championship confirmed that belief."

One other item to include. There is no question that Jim Tressel and his coaching staff turned in a coaching job for the ages in 2002. The on-the-field success of this ball club certainly was a reflection of this truly great coaching staff. But it would also seem proper at this time to mention former Ohio State football coach John Cooper. Much like Butch Davis at Miami, Cooper and assistants, who are no longer part of the program, recruited many of these players who were part of the Buckeyes' national championship team at Ohio State.

What's Next?

What will happen when the Buckeyes hit the field to begin the 2003 season to defend their national title? Almost right away after the Fiesta Bowl people were asking if the Buckeyes would be preseason number one going into the season of their title defense.

The hard question to answer, really, is: how will winning the national title affect this program in the future?

Whenever Ohio State has taken the football field, the targets on their backs have always been big because they're Ohio State, because of the success of teams long before 2002, and because of all of the factors that make the Buckeye tradition so strong. In a day and age when dynasties don't exist in sports as they did when Ohio State controlled the college football landscape in the fifties, sixties, and early seventies, opponents still get geared up to turn in their best performances when they face the Scarlet and Gray. That was never more obvious than when we think about the results of some of the games when the Buckeyes were fortunate to escape with wins in 2002 en route to this championship. All of this in a season in which the Buckeyes weren't even the preseason favorite to win the conference.

Certainly what occurred will have its expected impact on recruiting, sales of merchandise, and added attention, if that's possible, to Ohio State games on radio and TV—and also greater expectations. In the months since January 3, one theme has been voiced numerous times: The bar has been raised. And keep in mind that bar, for Ohio State, has always been a high one.

For all who witnessed the Ohio State Buckeyes of 2002, there are many memories. Many moments that can be looked at as "crucial plays." The debut of Maurice Clarett in the season opener against Texas Tech. The decisive win over Pac-10 favorite Washington State in Columbus. Chris Gamble's interceptions in the Penn State and Wisconsin games. Will Allen saving the Michigan and Cincinnati games with interceptions. Craig Krenzel hitting his money man, Michael Jenkins, with big passes at Purdue and Wisconsin, and against Miami. Maurice Hall scoring game-winning touchdowns at Illinois and against Michigan. The defense harassing Illinois and Miami on the final plays of those thrillers. Andy Groom's well-placed punts, and Mike Nugent's record-setting kicking season. There are many other moments that can be thrown in there. Heaven knows this team provided enough of them. Everyone who followed this team during the 2002 season will have many memories of moments they thought were crucial parts of this team's success.

But I would like to single out the group of 13 seniors who provided leadership to this championship team and how they did it in a very dedicated and purposeful manner. Certainly there were seniors like Mike Doss, Matt Wilhelm, Andy Groom, Kenny Peterson, Donnie Nickey, and Cie Grant who got their share of headlines and made their big plays. But there were also seniors who gained very little attention and fanfare, but delivered when they were called upon in their own ways, whether it was during a game, in practice, or in even more private circumstances that no one would know about. David Thompson, Chris Vance, Chris Conwell, Jack Tucker, Jeremy Uhlenhake, Mike Stafford, and Scott Kuhnhein all made their contributions in this special effort. Their fingerprints are part of a time in Ohio State football that provided one of the most exciting runs to an unbeaten regular season.

These seniors also were part of what will go down in history as the most exciting college football championship game to date in division 1-A. They were part of something truly special in a time when sports has not always been about good, positive headlines. College sports have not been exempt from their share of dark moments. These 13 seniors went through a stage in which there were many questions about the leadership of Ohio State football and the examples being set at times by some of the upperclassmen. They rose to the challenges they faced, both off and on the field. Jim Tressell and his coaching staff deserve all the credit in the world, but certainly they would be the first to tell you that you have to have willing pupils to teach. I hearken back to a line my late father used to use when it came time to impress upon my siblings and me that it didn't matter how much help you got with something, you had to be willing to work for any achievement yourself. He would say, "Buy them books, buy them books, and all they do is eat the pages!" This Ohio State team read the book, studied it over and over, and lived by it!

They had the success they enjoyed because they got great teaching from their coaching staff, they got stellar leadership from their captains, and they had faith in one another. Even when they faced the darkest of moments on the field, even when it seemed that the national title might have slipped away from them in the first overtime of the Fiesta Bowl, they never gave up. We all understood, even if we didn't want to agree, why many who didn't watch this team on a regular basis didn't expect them to reach a national title game, let alone have a chance to win it. But one of the great things about sports is the threat and the success that an underdog can bring to an event. Who imagined that in 1966 Texas Western had any shot of beating Kentucky in the NCAA basketball championship game?

Who honestly thought the Cincinnati Reds had a shot against the mighty Oakland Athletics in the 1990 World Series? Of recent vintage, what chance did anyone give the New England Patriots to defeat the St. Louis Rams in 2002?

And who thought the 2002 Ohio State Buckeyes would be college football's national champions?

THEY DID!

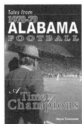

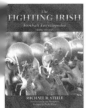

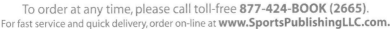